THE KINGFISHER ILLUSTRATED HORSE&PONY ENCYCLOPEDIA

WRITTEN BY
Sandy Ransford

PHOTOGRAPHED BY
Bob Langrish

KINGFISHER
BOSTON

KINGFISHER

a Houghton Mifflin Company imprint
222 Berkeley Street
Boston, Massachusetts 02116
www.houghtonmifflinbooks.com

First published in 2004
2 4 6 8 10 9 7 5 3 1

1TR/0204/TOM/CSN/150MA

LIBRARY OF CONGRESS CATALOGING-IN-PUBLICATION DATA
Ransford, Sandy.
Kingfisher illustrated horse & pony encyclopedia/Sandy P. G.
Ransford—1st ed.
p. cm.
Includes bibliographical references and index.
1. Horses—Encyclopedias, Juvenile. 2. Horsemanship—
Encyclopedias,
Juvenile. 3. Ponies—Encyclopedias, Juvenile. [1. Horses. 2.
Horsemanship.
3. Ponies.] I. Title: Horse and pony encyclopedia. II. Title.
SF302.R365 2004
636.1'003–dc22
2003027293

ISBN 0-7534-5781-4

FOR KINGFISHER
Publishing manager: Melissa Fairley
Coordinating editor: Caitlin Doyle
Art director: Mike Davis
Picture manager: Cee Weston-Baker
Production manager: Nancy Roberts
DTP coordinator: Sarah Pfitzner
DTP operator: Primrose Burton
Artwork archivists: Wendy Allison, Jenny Lord
Proofreader: Sheila Clewley
U.S. consultant: Lesley Ward

PROJECT TEAM
Project director: Julian Holland
Designers: Marcus Andrews, Nigel White
Photographer: Bob Langrish

Printed in China

Contents

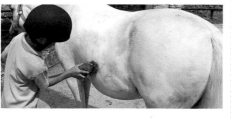

Introducing the horse

Przewalski's Horse
This horse, which was discovered living wild in Mongolia in the 1870s, looks a lot like the primitive ancestors of today's horses and ponies.

Generous, willing, and patient, horses have been serving people well for thousands of years. We have ridden them, driven them, used them to pull heavy loads and to plow our fields, and fought battles from their backs. Incredibly strong but very gentle, they look to us for leadership, which is why they allow us to tell them what to do. For centuries they were our only form of transportation. Now we use horses and ponies mostly for pleasure, so we owe it to them to learn as much as we can about them, to try and understand them, and to treat them kindly.

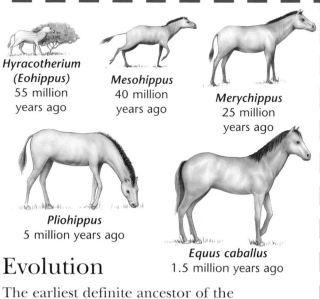

*Hyracotherium
(Eohippus)*
55 million
years ago

Mesohippus
40 million
years ago

Merychippus
25 million
years ago

Pliohippus
5 million years ago

Equus caballus
1.5 million years ago

Evolution

The earliest definite ancestor of the horse lived around 55 million years ago in North America. Similar in size to a fox, it had four toes on its front feet and three on its hind feet and lived in marshy areas where it fed on vegetation. Over time the horse got larger, and its extra toes disappeared. Its teeth adapted to grazing, and the position of its eyes changed to give it wider vision.

Domestication and training

The horse has come a long way since its wild ancestry. A dressage horse, for example, is trained to obey the slightest movement of its rider's hands, legs, and weight. An event horse is encouraged by its rider to clear fences it would never attempt on its own. A police horse will move toward a noisy and unruly crowd. A knowledgeable and sympathetic rider can calm a horse's fears and prevent it from obeying its instinct to run away from danger.

Wild ponies in Exmoor
Ponies and horses naturally live in family groups—mares, foals, and young animals—with the herd stallion. Being on their own is unnatural and makes them nervous.

In the show ring
The horse is such a remarkable animal that it can be trained to excel in a wide range of activities, like this beautifully turned out show horse.

Natural world of horses

Horses and ponies are herd animals. They form small groups, and within the groups there are particular friendships and sometimes dislikes. In the wild horses spend up to 20 hours each day grazing, roaming freely in search of food. When they rest, at least one group member stands guard over its sleeping companions.

Domesticated horses

A pony can feel unhappy if it is kept on its own. If there are no other horses or ponies around, other animals, like sheep and cows, make good company. The life of a domesticated pony is not natural, so try to give your pony as much freedom as possible.

Mutual grooming

Wild and domesticated ponies often groom each other if they are friends. They scratch each other's necks, withers, or backs with their front teeth. This is their way of strengthening a friendship.

Flehmen reaction

A pony may curl up its top lip when it senses an unusual smell or taste. This strange action lets it draw air across special sense organs in the roof of its mouth so that it can analyze the smell.

A horse's body language

Ears pricked forward show that a horse is interested in what is going on and expects good things to happen.

One ear to the side shows that the pony is distracted by something other than its main object of interest.

Ears laid back show anger or fear. The pony is warning you—or another pony—that it may kick or bite.

Herd animals

In the wild horses and ponies, such as these Mustangs, live in small family groups. These groups consist of one stallion, a few mares and their foals, and young animals that remain until they form herds of their own.

Fighting talk

In a group of horses and ponies each animal has a position in a hierarchy, and squabbles occur if one horse tries to challenge for a higher position. In the wild stallions fight off rivals, biting and striking out with a foreleg or swinging their hindquarters around, ready to kick. But horses and ponies threaten each other much more than they actually fight. Usually ears laid back and an outstretched neck are enough to frighten away another pony.

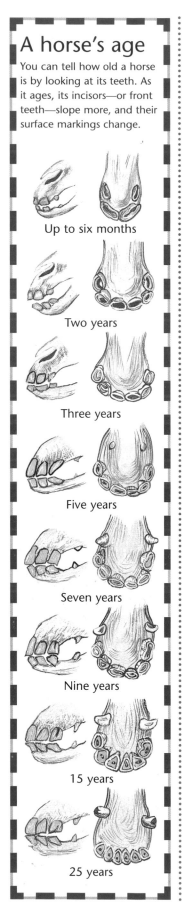

A horse's age

You can tell how old a horse is by looking at its teeth. As it ages, its incisors—or front teeth—slope more, and their surface markings change.

Up to six months

Two years

Three years

Five years

Seven years

Nine years

15 years

25 years

Life cycle of the horse

Horses and ponies can continue growing until they are five or six years old—the time when they are mature. Before that time their bones are not strong enough for hard work. As they grow older, the shape of their teeth, as well as the markings on them, change. Horses are considered old from their late teens, but many continue to work happily into their 20s. They may live for 30 years or more.

In-foal mare

"In foal" means that a mare is pregnant. She carries her foal for 11 months, and toward the end of that time she looks very round. Her change in shape is especially noticeable from the front and back.

Newborn foal

When a foal is born, the mare licks it clean. The foal usually gets to its feet within around one hour, when it will take its first drink of milk. Although they are wobbly at first, foals born in the wild can walk, trot, and even gallop alongside their mothers a few hours after their birth.

Early days

For the first 12 months of its life a horse or pony is called a foal. Long legs enable foals to move quickly. Foals suckle until they are four to six months old, but long before that they start nibbling grass.

Yearling

Long legged and lanky, a yearling is between 12 and 24 months old.

Two year old

By two it begins to look like an adult, although it is still immature.

Four year old

At four a horse is almost mature and is ready to begin its working life.

Ten year old

Between around five and 12 years old a horse is in its prime. Horses that compete are at their peak during these years.

Old horse

Around 20 years old there may be dips in its back and in front of its withers. Its legs and joints may become thicker.

Domestication of the horse

Early humans hunted horses for food. Around 6,000 years ago they began to herd horses and may also have ridden them. Fossilized teeth seem to show that horses had bits in their mouths 500 years before the invention of the wheel. Horse-drawn chariots were used in battle, as well as for racing and hunting wild animals. Cavalry gradually replaced the charioteers, and they started the tradition of handling horses from their left sides. Whether ridden or driven, horses became vital for transportation and for work on farms. It has only been more recently that we have used them mostly for recreation.

Chariot racing

Chariot racing was a popular sport among the aristocracy in Roman times. This stone relief shows a team of horses racing in the Circus Maximus in Rome, Italy, and dates back to the A.D. 100s.

Cave paintings

In Altamira in northern Spain horses are among the animals that appear in cave paintings dating back to between 15000 and 10000 B.C.

Jousting

Medieval knights fought battles on horseback and practiced their skills in jousting tournaments. They charged at each other with raised lances (spears), with each knight aiming to knock the other knight off his horse.

Transportation

The picture below shows the Duke of Beaufort's mail coach in London, England, in 1841. Passengers on mail coaches paid five old pence per mile for an inside seat and two-and-a-half old pence per mile for a seat on top.

Napoléon

Because soldiers, including Napoléon Bonaparte, carried swords on their left sides, they had to mount from this side. They handled their horses from the left, and we still follow this tradition today.

High school

This horse is performing an artificial pace called the Spanish Trot. Its forelegs are lifted up very high and stretched out straight in front.

Types of horses

Horses and ponies vary in type from the large, heavily built, slow-moving draft horse to the slender, fast Thoroughbred; from the solid, weight-carrying cob to the elegant show pony. Types are usually a mixture of different breeds, although many are specially bred. For example, a heavy horse crossed with a Thoroughbred will produce a horse that is capable of carrying a large, heavy rider.

Driving types

Horses and ponies suitable for driving tend to have straight shoulders—on which the collar of the harness fits well—and upright pasterns. They often have high action, which looks good when they are pulling a carriage but would be very uncomfortable on a riding horse.

Heavy horses
This type of horse is massively built. Their bones are huge, and they have enormous muscles. They are capable of pulling very heavy weights.

Carriage horses
These types must also be strong, but they are lighter, more elegantly built, and often high-stepping. A matching pair is highly prized.

Riding types

A riding horse or pony has to be strong enough to carry its rider but narrow enough to ride. Sloping shoulders give a horse a long, low stride, which is comfortable for the rider. Sloping pasterns also make a horse a good ride, while powerful hindquarters and long hind legs give jumping ability.

Show pony
A show pony or horse has all the best points of a riding pony or horse. It must be beautiful, have good conformation and paces, and behave perfectly.

Cob
A cob is a quiet riding horse, with short legs and a deep body. Traditionally it was ridden by elderly, often heavy, riders. A cob's mane is usually roached.

Polo ponies
These are actually small horses. They have to be fast, able to start, stop, and turn quickly, and must obey their rider's commands instantly.

Working hunter pony
This is more solidly built and plainer than the classic show pony. As well as being a good general riding pony, it must be able to gallop and jump.

Points of a horse

The points of a horse or pony are the visible parts of its anatomy. Each has a name, which you will find useful to learn because they will help you understand magazines and books you read and instructions you may be given when you take riding lessons. By becoming familiar with these terms, you will learn more about horses and ponies and be better able to talk to other people interested in horses. You will be able to talk about pony care and discuss any problems with a vet.

Conformation

Conformation means the way in which a horse or pony is put together. It varies according to type and breed, but the body should look in proportion. A small head; large, clear eyes; sloping shoulders and pasterns; a good circumference of bone below the knee; a short back, and powerful hindquarters are considered good conformation.

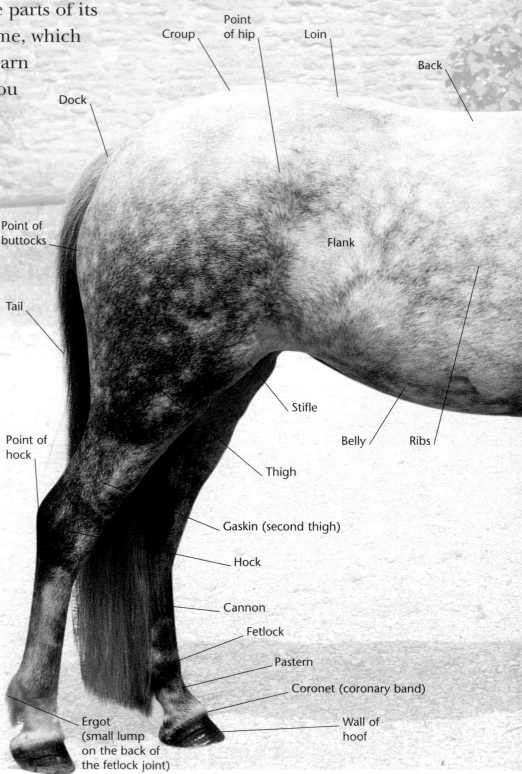

Croup

Point of hip

Loin

Back

Dock

Point of buttocks

Flank

Tail

Stifle

Belly

Ribs

Point of hock

Thigh

Gaskin (second thigh)

Hock

Cannon

Fetlock

Pastern

Coronet (coronary band)

Ergot (small lump on the back of the fetlock joint)

Wall of hoof

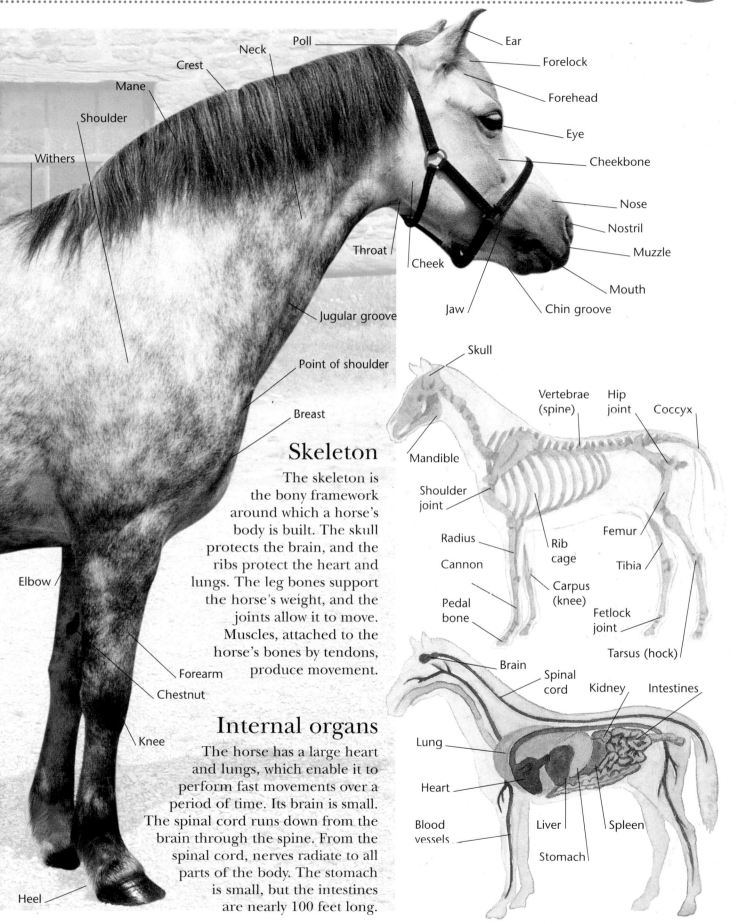

Poll

Neck

Crest

Mane

Shoulder

Withers

Ear

Forelock

Forehead

Eye

Cheekbone

Nose

Nostril

Muzzle

Throat

Cheek

Mouth

Jugular groove

Jaw

Chin groove

Point of shoulder

Breast

Skull

Vertebrae (spine)

Hip joint

Coccyx

Mandible

Shoulder joint

Skeleton

The skeleton is the bony framework around which a horse's body is built. The skull protects the brain, and the ribs protect the heart and lungs. The leg bones support the horse's weight, and the joints allow it to move. Muscles, attached to the horse's bones by tendons, produce movement.

Radius

Cannon

Pedal bone

Rib cage

Carpus (knee)

Femur

Tibia

Fetlock joint

Tarsus (hock)

Elbow

Forearm

Chestnut

Knee

Internal organs

The horse has a large heart and lungs, which enable it to perform fast movements over a period of time. Its brain is small. The spinal cord runs down from the brain through the spine. From the spinal cord, nerves radiate to all parts of the body. The stomach is small, but the intestines are nearly 100 feet long.

Brain

Spinal cord

Kidney

Intestines

Lung

Heart

Blood vessels

Liver

Spleen

Stomach

Heel

Colors

The color of a horse's or pony's coat depends on the amount of pigment, or natural coloring, in its skin. Almost all horses and ponies have dark skin, except where they have white markings such as on the face and lower legs, where the skin is pink. Only rare, pure-white horses called albinos have pink skin all over. Most horses and ponies that we think are white are actually gray. They have dark skin, which you can see on their muzzles.

As horses age

As horses and ponies grow older their color may change. Grays are born dark and gradually become lighter, until they look white. Some grays develop dark, usually brown, flecks. This color is called "flea-bitten gray." Browns, blacks, bays, and chestnuts may have some white hairs in their coats, manes, and tails.

Bay is a rich, reddish-brown coat color with a black mane, tail, and lower legs.

Flea-bitten gray is a light gray color with dark, usually brown, flecks.

Bright bay is lighter than bay with more yellow in the coat color.

Brown is dark brown, often with paler areas. Also called dark bay.

Dapple gray has black and white hairs that form rings called dapples.

Black is black all over, including the mane and tail. Pure black is rare.

Eye color

The color of a horse's or pony's eyes, like that of its coat, is determined by the amount of pigment it has. As most horses and ponies have dark skin, most also have brown eyes. But occasionally, as with the albino and sometimes with spotted horses, the eyes are light-colored. In the Appaloosa breed the white of the eye can be seen all the time.

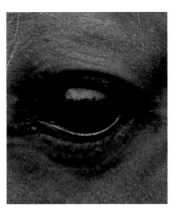

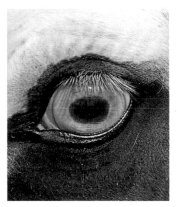

Brown eyes
The iris of the eye is dark brown. The white of the eye, which surrounds the iris, can be seen only when the horse is frightened or angry.

Wall eyes
In a "wall eye" the iris is bluish- or pinkish-white. This unusual color does not affect the horse's sight. These are also called china, blue, or glass eyes.

Hoof color

The color of the horn of a horse's or pony's hooves is related to the color of its coat on the leg just above the hoof. Black or dark colored legs have dark hooves, which are called "blue." Where there are white socks or other leg markings the hooves are light-colored and are called "white." A horse may have hooves that are different colors.

Blue hoof and white hoof
The pony's leg shown on the left of the picture is dark and has a blue hoof. The leg on the right has a white sock, so the hoof is also white.

Striped hooves
Horse and pony breeds with spotted coats, such as the Appaloosa, have striped hooves (above). Light and dark stripes run up and down the feet.

Liver chestnut
is a darker chestnut, like the color of raw liver.

Chestnut
is red-gold or ginger, often with a darker or lighter mane and tail.

Blue roan
is black with white hairs through it, giving a bluish color.

Strawberry roan is chestnut with white hairs through it.

Yellow dun
is a yellowish, cookie-colored coat with black points.

Skewbald
is brown-and-white patches all over. Also called part-colored.

Piebald
is black-and-white patches all over. Also called part-colored.

Spotted is dark spots on a white coat or white spots on a dark coat.

Markings

The word "markings" means all the patches and stripes on a horse or pony that are a different color from its coat. These markings are usually white and appear on the face and legs. The shape and size of the markings varies a lot between different horses, and they are recorded and used to help identify the animal.

Face markings

Marks on the face are white and usually appear on the front of the face. These marks may cover a large area or a very small one and can be many different shapes. To make it easier to describe these marks and record them, different types of markings are given special names.

Blaze is a fairly broad white band down the face.

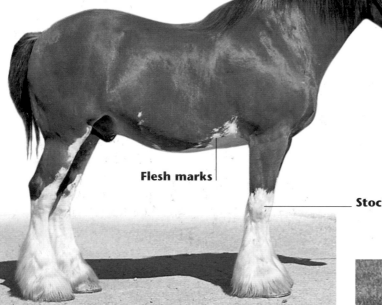

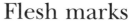

Blaze

Flesh marks

Stocking

Flesh marks

White patches on the underside of a horse's belly and on its flanks are called "flesh marks." These marks are often seen on Clydesdale horses (left). Sometimes horses have white marks on their backs or in other places. These are usually the result of an injury or wound and are called "acquired marks."

Leg markings

Leg markings are mostly white and are usually called "socks" or "stockings," but there may also be dark marks. When markings are written down to help identify a horse, they are described very carefully. For example, a certificate may say "white midpastern to coronet" or "white to midcannon."

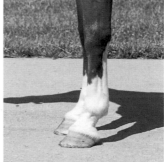

Socks are white marks that go above the fetlock but not as far as the knee or hock.

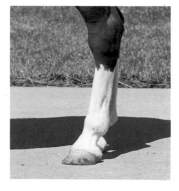

Stockings are white marks that reach and sometimes cover the knee or hock.

Stripe is a narrow band of white down the face.

Star is a white mark of any shape on the forehead.

Snip is a patch of white on the nose between the nostrils.

Whorl is a ring of hair that grows in different directions.

Eel stripe

Primitive breeds, such as Przewalski's Horse (right) and Fjord and Highland ponies, often have a black stripe running along their backs from the mane to the tail. This is called an "eel" or "dorsal" stripe and is usually seen with a dun-colored coat.

Eel stripe

Bald face

A very broad white blaze that goes all the way across the front of a horse's face is called a "bald face." It reaches as far as the eyes and covers the horse's muzzle.

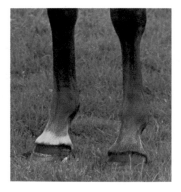

White coronets cover the area just above the hoof, which is called the coronet.

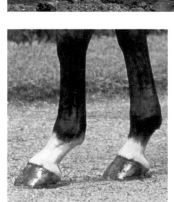

White pasterns cover the pastern area between the hoof and the fetlock joint.

Ermine marks are small, dark spots on white socks next to dark marks on the hooves.

Zebra marks are horizontal dark stripes on the lower legs seen in ancient breeds.

What is a breed?

Horses and ponies vary in shape and size. Some belong to a particular breed. This means that they share the same characteristics as other horses or ponies of the same breed. Horse breeds are divided into groups called coldblood, hotblood, and warmblood. The pony breeds are not usually classified in this way.

Coldbloods

Belgian Drafts (above) are typical coldblood horses. Coldbloods come from northern Europe, where the cool, damp weather produces plenty of rich grazing. This makes the horses bred there large and very strong.

Warmbloods

Warmblood breeds were produced by crossing hotbloods and coldbloods. This horse (left) is a warmblood, although it does not belong to a specific breed. It is a "type" called a heavyweight hunter. Types of horses are defined by the kind of work they do.

Hotbloods

The Anglo-Arab (above) is a fine example of the beauty, grace, and elegance of the hotblood breeds. Hotbloods originally came from the Middle East and North Africa, where poor grazing and the extreme climate produced a light, tough, fast horse.

Ponies

Ponies stand up to 14.2hh (57 in.), and most, like the Icelandics (right), are warmbloods. Ponies have shorter legs than horses, and they are stronger in relation to their size. They are sturdy, tough, and independent.

Hotblood
horses

Hotblood horses are ancient and very pure breeds that have had an enormous influence on the breeding of almost all other horses and ponies. Lightly built, with fine skins and thin coats, they are high-spirited and courageous and make ideal horses for experienced riders.

Arabian

The Arabian is probably the oldest and most beautiful breed of horse in the world. It has played an important part in the development of horse and pony breeds in almost every country. With its high head and tail carriage, great presence, and floating action, an Arabian horse is instantly recognizable. Although it is a small horse, the Arabian is strong and is famous for its stamina.

Arabian head

The head is small and elegant, with a "dished," or concave, profile. The neck has a high crest. The angle at which the neck joins the head, called the mitbah, is seen only in this breed.

An Arabian's back is short and compact because it has fewer bones in its spine than other horses. The joints of the legs are flat, and the pasterns are sloping. The chest is broad, and the feet are hard and well-formed.

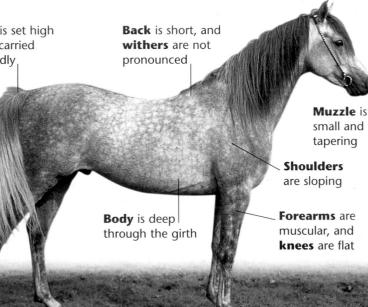

Tail is set high and carried proudly

Back is short, and **withers** are not pronounced

Muzzle is small and tapering

Shoulders are sloping

Body is deep through the girth

Forearms are muscular, and **knees** are flat

Mare and foal
An Arabian horse is high-spirited and courageous, but it also has a kind and gentle nature, making it easy to handle. Arabian foals are lively and inquisitive.

Desert horses

Arabians were first bred in the deserts of the Arabian peninsula, where they have existed for at least 4,000 years. Poor food and harsh conditions have produced a small, fast horse that is strong and tough. Arabians are raced over more than 280 mi. (150km) and are regarded as prized possessions by their owners.

Key facts

- **Place of origin**
  The Arabian peninsula, now called Saudi Arabia

- **Height**
  14.2–15hh (57–59 in.) or larger

- **Color**
  Mostly chestnut, bay, and gray; brown and black are seen rarely

- **Uses**
  General riding; showing; endurance riding; specialist racing; also as a cross with other breeds to produce quality show horses and ponies

- **Characteristics**
  Courageous and gentle

Thoroughbred

The Thoroughbred is the fastest breed of horse in the world. It was produced in England in the 1600s and 1700s by crossing three Arabian stallions—the Darley Arabian, the Godolphin Arabian, and the Byerley Turk—with English mares. Thoroughbreds have developed into perfect racehorses. They have also had a huge effect on horse breeding throughout the world. They succeed at all types of equestrian sports and make good riding horses.

Thoroughbred breeding

Thoroughbred horses are very valuable. Those to be used for racing are called bloodstock and are bred from former racehorses on special stud farms. Young horses are turned out together in paddocks until they are old enough to begin their training.

On the gallops

When Thoroughbred racehorses have become used to carrying a rider and obeying commands, they are trained on stretches of land called gallops. Here they can gallop for long distances. They usually exercise in groups, called strings, supervised by their trainers.

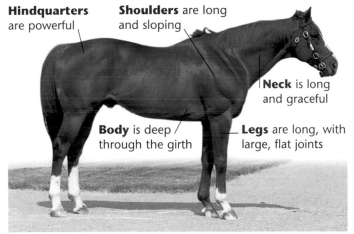

Hindquarters are powerful

Shoulders are long and sloping

Neck is long and graceful

Body is deep through the girth

Legs are long, with large, flat joints

Steeplechasing

Thoroughbreds compete in both flat racing and racing over fences, which is called steeplechasing. The gray horse above right is Desert Orchid, one of the most successful recent steeplechasers. He is shown here racing in Cheltenham, England, in 1990.

Eventing
Many horses that compete in eventing are either pure- or partbred Thoroughbreds.

Many people believe that this breed is the perfect riding horse. Its sloping shoulders and long pasterns produce long, low strides, making it comfortable to ride. Its powerful quarters give it great speed. It is light and graceful, yet strong, and has great stamina.

Key facts

- **Place of origin**
  England

- **Height**
  15.2–16.2hh
  (61–66 in.)

- **Color**
  Brown, bay, black, chestnut, gray; always solid colors

- **Uses**
  Racing; riding; showing; dressage; show jumping; eventing

- **Characteristics**
  Fast and courageous but also highly strung and sometimes difficult to handle

Anglo-Arab

Withers are higher than Arabian's

Quarters are strong

Head has Arabian's gentle expression

Legs have plenty of bone

Body is deep through the girth

The Anglo-Arab is a cross between the Arabian and the Thoroughbred. It has the beauty and intelligence of the Arabian and the size and speed of the Thoroughbred. Although the breed originated in England, much of its development took place in France.

Endurance riding

Anglo-Arabs, as well as purebred and partbred Arabians, compete very successfully in long-distance endurance rides. The horses must be extremely fit and have great stamina because they may have to travel up to 50 mi. (80km) per day at an average speed of 9 mph (14–15km/h). Some endurance rides last for more than one day.

Its head is straighter in profile than the Arabian's, and the horse looks more like a Thoroughbred because of its greater size. Its long legs enable it to move with great speed. Its size means that it does very well in eventing and show jumping, as well as in dressage.

Key facts

- **Height**
  15.2–16.2hh
  (61–66 in.)

- **Color**
  Bay, chestnut, brown, gray

- **Uses**
  Riding; endurance; dressage; show jumping

Barb

The Barb comes from Morocco, in North Africa, and is one of the world's oldest breeds. Although it is not beautiful, the Barb is sound and tough and has great stamina. It is capable of great speed over short distances.

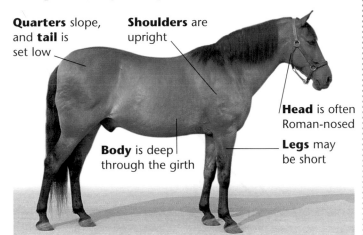

Quarters slope, and **tail** is set low

Shoulders are upright

Head is often Roman-nosed

Body is deep through the girth

Legs may be short

Mane and **tail** are thick and full

Head shape

The Barb is such an ancient breed that its skull shape is similar to that of primitive horses. Its head is quite large and plain and does not have the Arabian's grace and beauty.

The Barb, like the Arabian, has had a great influence on horse breeding throughout the world. The Spanish Horse, from which many horse and pony breeds were developed, was itself descended from the Barb. The breed is the traditional mount of the Berbers of North Africa.

Akhal-Teke

Bred in the deserts of Turkmenistan, north of Iran, the Akhal-Teke is an unusual-looking horse. It has a long, lean body and neck and long legs. It is capable of great feats of endurance and is used for long-distance riding, racing, jumping, and dressage.

The Akhal-Teke has been bred for thousands of years. It is spirited and courageous, hardy and strong. This breed stands around 15.2hh (61 in.) and has a fine coat and a silky mane and tail. The most prized color is this unique metallic golden dun.

Head is elegant

Back is long

Neck is slender and carried high

Body is narrow

Hocks are set high up

Legs are long, and **feet** are small

Good jumper

Because of its great stamina, the Akhal-Teke is mainly known for its success in long-distance riding and racing. But it is also a good jumper and competes successfully in both show jumping and dressage.

Coldblood horses

Coldblood breeds are large, heavy, and very strong. Many have existed for thousands of years. They were bred for farmwork and for pulling heavy loads. Coldbloods have calm and docile natures. Most have "feather"—hair—around their feet.

Ardennais

This heavy draft horse has been bred in the Ardennes region, on the borders of France and Belgium, for hundreds of years. It is probably descended from medieval warhorses. In the 1800s the Ardennais developed into two main types—a massive farm horse and a more lightweight animal.

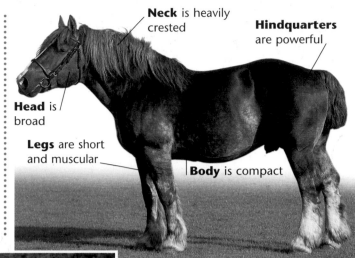

Neck is heavily crested

Hindquarters are powerful

Head is broad

Legs are short and muscular

Body is compact

Crowd pullers

Ardennais are not often used for farming today, but these good-natured, easy-to-handle horses are still popular at shows. This pair, pulling a farm wagon, are the typical red roan color.

Ardennais stand between 15 and 16hh (59–64 in.). They are tough, hardy animals and are able to withstand a harsh climate and survive on poor food. Ardennais horses are often roan in color, although they may also be bay, chestnut, or gray.

Hindquarters are very muscular

Neck has a large crest and a fine, silky mane

Head is elegant

Shoulders are powerful

Legs are huge and carry little feather

Despite its size, the Boulonnais is an elegant horse owing to its Arabian and Barb ancestors. It is usually gray but is also sometimes black, roan, bay, or chestnut. This horse is well-proportioned and has a fine coat and thick, silky mane and tail hair. It stands between 16 and 17hh (64–68 in.).

Boulonnais

The Boulonnais comes from the area around Boulogne in northeast France. Two types of Boulonnais were bred—one was a heavy farm worker, and the other was a lighter, faster horse called a *mareyeur* (meaning "fish seller"). This horse was used for transporting fish from the coast to Paris.

Fast action

The Boulonnais can move faster than most heavy horses and has lower knee action. Some still work on farms, but to ensure the breed does not die out, the French government breeds Boulonnais.

Percheron

This powerful breed comes from La Perche in northern France. Its ancestors carried knights who wore heavy armor. In the 1700s the Percheron was crossed with the Arabian, giving it greater quality and better action. These horses are clean-legged, a great advantage when they work on the land.

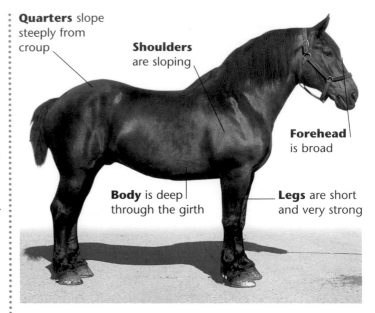

Quarters slope steeply from croup

Shoulders are sloping

Forehead is broad

Body is deep through the girth

Legs are short and very strong

Key facts

- **Place of origin**
  Normandy, France
- **Height**
  16.1–17.2hh (64–69 in.)
- **Color**
  Gray or black
- **Uses**
  Farmwork; driving

One of the tallest horses that has ever lived was a Percheron. It stood 21hh (83 in.), though not many of them are as large as that. Percherons are broad, compact, and very strong, with sturdy legs and good feet. The breed has a more elegant appearance, lower action, and a finer head than most heavy breeds because of its Arabian blood.

Carriage horses

Although some Percherons still work on the land, they are also popular as carriage horses. Despite being so large, they have a low, free action and move easily. They are docile and work well.

Suffolk

Suffolk foal
Suffolks mature early and live for a long time. This foal may start its working life at two years old and continue for many years. Suffolks are valuable as both farm horses and draft horses in towns.

O ften called the Suffolk Punch, this is the most purebred of all of Great Britain's heavy horses. All Suffolks are descended from one stallion called the Horse of Ufford, which was born in 1768. The Suffolk is stocky, with short legs, and is always chestnut in color. Some Suffolks are used for farmwork, but the breed is now mostly seen in the showring.

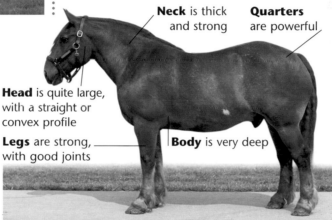

Neck is thick and strong

Quarters are powerful

Head is quite large, with a straight or convex profile

Legs are strong, with good joints

Body is very deep

The Suffolk has a round, barrel-shaped body on short, strong legs. Its chest is wide, and it has a thick neck with low withers. Despite its bulk, the horse moves freely and has an energetic trot. It has a friendly and docile temperament and is easy to handle.

Key facts

- **Place of origin**
  Suffolk, England

- **Height**
  16–16.3hh
  (64–66 in.)

- **Color**
  Always chestnut, with no white markings except on the face

Farm horse

The Suffolk was bred to work on farms in eastern England. The lack of feather on its legs is an advantage, as it means that the heavy clay soil does not cling to them. Suffolks do not need a lot of food, which makes them inexpensive to keep.

Shire

Tall and extremely strong, the Shire is probably the heaviest of England's heavy horses. It can weigh up to 2,700 lbs. and may stand up to 17.2hh (69 in.). Its girth can measure up to 8 ft. The Shire gets its name from the English counties where it was bred (Derbyshire, Staffordshire, Lincolnshire, and Leicestershire). Shire horses often worked on farms. Many brewers also used them to pull carts called drays to deliver beer in cities.

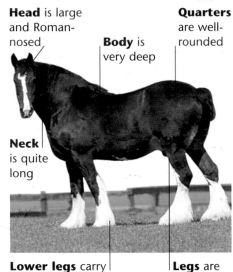

Knights' horse

In medieval times the Shire was called "the great horse of England." Its size and strength made it the ideal horse for carrying knights in armor, who could weigh up to 420 lbs. (190kg). This breed was also an all-around workhorse, employed on farms and wherever great pulling power was needed.

Plowing match

There are not many working Shire horses today, but they are often seen at plowing matches and shows. Their manes are braided with ribbons, and their bridles and harnesses gleam with polished brass. They are a magnificent sight, and their strength and gentleness are much admired.

Head is large and Roman-nosed

Body is very deep

Quarters are well-rounded

Neck is quite long

Lower legs carry a lot of feather

Legs are very strong

This tall and extremely powerful horse is able to pull five times its own weight. A Shire is usually black, bay, brown, or gray in color. Its legs often have long white stockings, and the feather is fine and silky. Shires' tails are often cut short, which means that they lose their natural flyswatters.

Pleasant horse
The Shire has a broad forehead. Its large eyes have a sympathetic expression, which shows how gentle this breed can be. The face often has a broad white blaze that goes over the nose and the muzzle.

Neck is thick and arched

Key facts

- **Place of origin**
  The Midlands, in England
- **Height**
  16.2–17.2hh (66–69 in.)
- **Color**
  Bay, brown, black, or gray
- **Uses**
  As dray horses; for showing

Clydesdale

The Clydesdale is related to the Shire but is lighter in build. This breed comes from Scotland, where it was originally used for farmwork. Later it was used to pull various forms of transportation, including coal wagons. Today the Clydesdale is seen at shows and in plowing matches. It is also crossed with Thoroughbreds to produce heavyweight riding horses.

Clydesdales are usually bay, brown, black, or roan. They often have white markings that start at their feet and go right up the legs. Some cover part of the horse's belly, and the face may be mostly white too. These big horses stand around 16.2 to 17hh (66–67 in.).

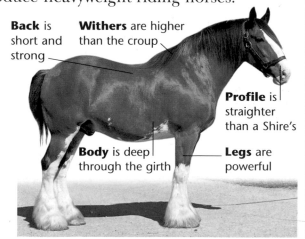

Back is short and strong

Withers are higher than the croup

Profile is straighter than a Shire's

Body is deep through the girth

Legs are powerful

Trade turnout
Beautifully decorated Clydesdales are often seen at shows, harnessed to brightly painted vehicles called trade turnouts.

Back is short and strong

Neck is short and thick

Hindquarters are strong

Expression is gentle

Body is deep and compact

Shoulders are massively muscled

Belgian Draft

This ancient breed dates back to Roman times and is also known as the Brabant and Brabançon. The Belgian Draft's ancestors were warhorses, and they helped create the Shire, Clydesdale, and possibly the Suffolk. The breeding of Belgian Drafts was carefully controlled to produce an impressive horse.

Standing 16 to 17hh (64–68 in.), the Belgian Draft is a compact, very strong horse. It is usually chestnut or red roan in color. This breed of horse is good-natured and intelligent. It is a popular breed in the United States, as well as in its native Belgium.

Still working

Today the Belgian Draft is not used much for farmwork, but it can still be seen working in harness. This pair is pulling a trolley through the streets of a small, European-style town in California.

Noriker

This Austrian breed dates back to the 1500s. Its name comes from the word "Noricum," which was a Roman province situated where Austria is now. The Noriker is related to the Haflinger and was bred to work on the farms and forests of the Austrian Alps. It is strong, hardworking, and easy to handle.

Mane and **tail** are often flaxen

Back is long

Nostrils are wide

Legs are strong and carry little feather

Girth is huge

Broad horse

The Noriker has a broad chest, and its girth measurement should not be less than 60 percent of its height. It has short, sturdy legs. This breed's tough constitution helps it withstand the harsh Alpine winters.

The Noriker stands between 16 and 17hh (64–67 in.) and is chestnut, brown, or black in color. Its legs are strong, and its action is longer and lower than that of many heavy breeds. It has a calm temperament, is surefooted, and is economical to keep.

Friesian

This attractive breed from the Netherlands was the mount of German and Friesian knights during the Crusades. It was used for farmwork and, in the 1800s, for trotting races. Friesians are still ridden, but they are used mostly as carriage horses. As they are black, they are often used for funerals.

Neck is arched and carried high

Quarters slope from croup

Expression is alert

Legs are quite long and well-feathered

Body is not very deep

Four-in-hand

Friesians are popular driving horses. They are very handsome, and they have a fast, high-stepping trot. This team, called a four-in-hand, is owned by Harrods, a famous department store in London, England.

Standing between 15 and 16hh (59–64 in.), the Friesian is black all over, though some may have a small white star on their forcheads. The horse is lighter in build than many heavy breeds. The Friesian has a good temperament and is easy to handle.

Neck is short and huge

Quarters slope steeply from the croup

Head has a straight profile

Legs carry a lot of feather

Shoulders are muscular

Legs have huge muscles

Dutch Draught

This breed is believed to be the most massively built of all European heavy draft horses. It was developed in the late 1800s and early 1900s from the Ardennais and native horses. The Royal Dutch Draught Horse Society controls its breeding. The result is a very heavy and powerful working horse.

The Dutch Draught stands around 16.3hh (66 in.) and is usually chestnut, bay, roan, gray, or black in color. Although it is very heavy, its action is free and active. This breed matures early and is long-lived. The Dutch Draught has a quiet nature and is a good worker.

Show horse

Today, Dutch Draughts are mostly seen in the showring, where they may drive a variety of carts. Some, however, are still used to pull vehicles around city streets, selling or advertising goods.

Warmblood horses

Most of the horse and pony breeds throughout the world are classed as warmbloods. Many types of horses and ponies also belong to this group. Warmblood horses include the highly successful German and Dutch competition horses and most of the American breeds.

Swedish Warmblood

Bred from Spanish, oriental, and Friesian horses in the 1600s, the Swedish Warmblood was a cavalry horse. Later the breed was crossed with Thoroughbreds, Trakehners, Hanoverians, and Arabians. Today it is a competition horse—its is good at jumping, eventing, and dressage.

Standing around 16.2 to 17hh (66–68 in.), the Swedish Warmblood is a big, athletic horse. It has powerful shoulders and quarters, strong legs, and good feet. Its calm temperament and sensible attitude help make it good at dressage. It can be any solid color.

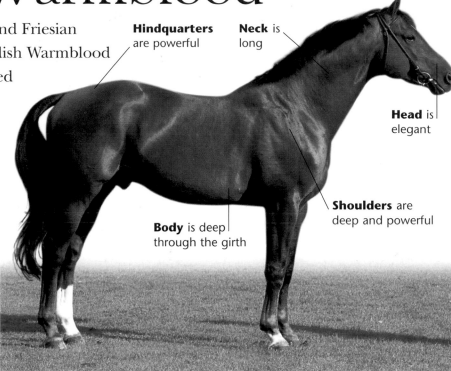

Hindquarters are powerful

Neck is long

Head is elegant

Shoulders are deep and powerful

Body is deep through the girth

Selle Français

The Selle Français (meaning "French saddle") was bred in Normandy, France, in the 1800s from native Norman horses and imported English Thoroughbreds. In the middle of the 1900s French Trotters, Thoroughbreds, Arabians, and Anglo-Arabs were used to develop the breed.

The Selle Français is a well-built horse, with strong legs and lots of muscle. Its body is quite long, and its withers are high. It stands around 16hh (64 in.). It is intelligent, with a calm temperament, and is agile and athletic. It may be any solid color.

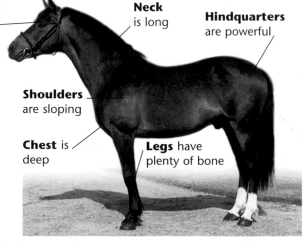

Expression shows its calm nature

Neck is long

Hindquarters are powerful

Shoulders are sloping

Chest is deep

Legs have plenty of bone

Good jumper

This horse excels at show jumping and eventing. It tackles difficult cross-country fences bravely and is good at dressage. It makes a good all-around riding horse. In France some Selle Français are bred especially for racing.

Competition breeds

Although many breeds and types of horses are good at dressage, eventing, and show jumping, the breeds described here are particularly well-known for this. They were produced by crossing farm and carriage horses with English Thoroughbreds. This made lighter, faster horses, while keeping the calmer nature of the heavier animals.

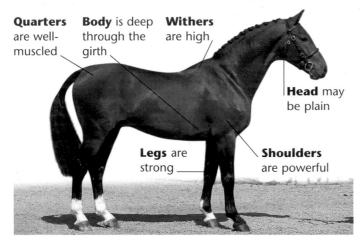

Quarters are well-muscled

Body is deep through the girth

Withers are high

Head may be plain

Legs are strong

Shoulders are powerful

Hanoverian

This breed was developed in the 1700s by crossing Holsteiners with local mares. This produced a strong horse that was used for farmwork. Trakehners and English Thoroughbreds were used to improve the breed and create a first-class competition horse.

Dressage champion
Strong, athletic, and with good action, this breed is superb at dressage. This picture shows Isabell Werth on Gigolo riding for Germany.

Quarters are muscular and powerful

Neck is long

Shoulders are sloping

Body is deep through the girth

Legs are strong, with plenty of bone

Dutch Warmblood

This breed was created in the 1900s by crossing the Gelderlander and the Groningen with the English Thoroughbred. It is possibly the most successful of the competition breeds. These horses are strong and athletic, with a calm temperament.

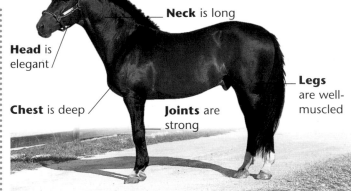

Neck is long

Head is elegant

Chest is deep

Joints are strong

Legs are well-muscled

Famous partnership
One of the most famous dressage partnerships of all time was Jennie Loriston-Clarke and Dutch Courage, here giving a demonstration of long-reining.

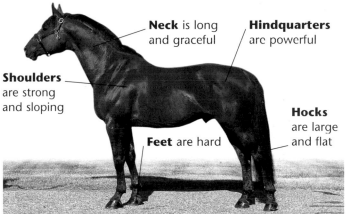

Marius, a highly successful Dutch Warmblood stallion, jumping in Calgary, Canada, in 1979

Holsteiner

Between the 1600s and 1800s Holsteiners were used as carriage horses. Since the 1800s they have been bred for riding. They are excellent at cross-country jumping and do well in dressage and show jumping.

Neck is long and graceful

Hindquarters are powerful

Shoulders are strong and sloping

Hocks are large and flat

Feet are hard

Trakehner

This breed began in East Prussia in the 1200s. Originally a carriage horse, it was crossed with Arabians and Thoroughbreds to produce cavalry horses. It is a first-class dressage, jumping, and eventing competitor.

Key facts

Dutch Warmblood	Holsteiner
• **Height** 15.3–16.3hh (62–66 in.)	• **Height** 16–17hh (64–68 in.)
• **Color** Any solid color	• **Color** Any solid color
Hanoverian	**Trakehner**
• **Height** 16–17hh (64–68 in.)	• **Height** 16–17.2hh (64–69 in.)
• **Color** Any solid color	• **Color** Any solid color

Oldenburg

The tallest and heaviest of the German warmblood breeds, the Oldenburg was bred in the 1600s as a coach horse. It was named after the area of Germany from which it came and the man who bred it, Count Anton von Oldenburg. Its ancestors include Friesian, Neapolitan, Spanish, Cleveland Bay, English Thoroughbred, and Norfolk Roadster horses. Today it is used for driving, dressage, and show jumping.

The Oldenburg is a large, powerfully built horse that stands between 16.2 and 17.2hh (66–69 in.). It is usually bay, brown, or black. It is good-natured and matures early, giving it a long working life.

Neck is very strong

Shoulders are like those of a coach horse

Quarters are well-developed

Profile may be straight or convex

Legs are quite short

Gelderlander

This breed comes from the Gelder area of the Netherlands, where it has been bred since the 1800s. Gelderlanders were then used mainly as carriage horses, but they were also expected to do light farmwork and double as riding horses. Their ancestors include the Oldenburg and the Thoroughbred.

The heavily built Gelderlander stands 15.2 to 16.2hh (61–66 in.) and is usually chestnut in color. It often has a wide white blaze on its face and white stockings on its legs. Although it is not thought of as a beautiful horse, it is very strong. The Gelderlander has a gentle, docile temperament, making it easy to handle.

Tail is set high

Shoulders are upright

Head is large and plain

Legs are strong

Carriage horses

Although Gelderlanders are no longer used for farmwork, they are still popular carriage horses and are used in driving competitions. They are also useful heavyweight riding horses, due to their size and strong build. These horses are not fast, but they are good jumpers.

Quarters slope from croup

Head has a straight or convex profile

Shoulders are good for harness work

Body is deep through the girth

French Trotter

This breed was developed in Normandy, France, in the 1800s to compete in the new sport of trotting. The first trotting racecourse in France opened in Cherbourg in 1836. The French Trotter's ancestors are the Norfolk Trotter, the English Thoroughbred, and horses from the Normandy region.

The French Trotter stands around 16.2hh (66 in.). It may be any solid color but is usually bay, brown, or chestnut. Strong and tough, with long legs, these horses have free-striding, active action, great stamina, and are willing workers.

Racing sulkies

French Trotters are generally raced in harness. The light, two-wheeled vehicles they pull are called sulkies. They are also raced under saddle. Some French Trotters are used for general riding and for breeding riding horses. They are good jumpers.

Camargue

The Camargue region of the Rhône delta in France is a bleak and windy area. Here, the wild Camargue horses have lived on poor grazing for thousands of years. Some are tamed and ridden by local cowboys to round up wild black bulls.

Wild white horses

Camargue ponies have been called the "wild white horses of the sea." They are small at 14hh (55 in.), very tough, and always white or gray in color. They look like the horses in ancient cave paintings.

Przewalski's Horse

In the late 1870s a Russian explorer named Nicolai Przewalski discovered a herd of pony-sized wild horses in the mountains of Mongolia, on the edge of the Gobi Desert. They looked similar to the primitive herds that once roamed Asia and became known as Przewalski's Horse. Also called the Mongolian or Asiatic Wild Horse, Przewalski's Horse and the Tarpan are two surviving strains of four types of primitive horses that existed 10,000 years ago.

The breed saved
Przewalski's Horse is now extinct in the wild, but it is preserved in zoos and private studs.

Stone Age horse

Between 16,000 and 27,000 years ago early humans painted animals on the walls of caves. Some of the pictures were of horses that looked like the animal we call Przewalski's Horse. Amazingly, this breed has hardly changed at all over this long period of time.

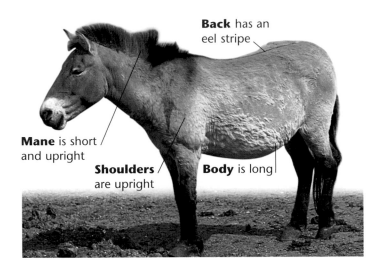

Back has an eel stripe

Mane is short and upright

Shoulders are upright

Body is long

Key facts

Przewalski's Horse	Tarpan
• **Height** 12–14.2hh (48–57 in.)	• **Height** Around 13hh (52 in.)
• **Color** Yellow dun, with black points	• **Color** Mouse dun, brown

Przewalski's Horse has similar features to primitive horses. The body is dun and has black points, and the legs may have zebra stripes. On the back is a black line called an eel stripe. The mane grows upright, and there is little or no forelock. The muzzle and the areas around the eyes are pale in color.

Face-to-face
Przewalski's Horses have large, plain heads with a convex or straight profile. Their eyes are set high up, so their heads look long.

Tarpan

The Tarpan originally lived in Russia and in Central and Eastern Europe. The breed was domesticated, but in the 1800s it became extinct. In the 1930s a Polish professor named Vetulani found ponies living in Polish forests that were like the ancient breed. With careful breeding, he recreated the Tarpan.

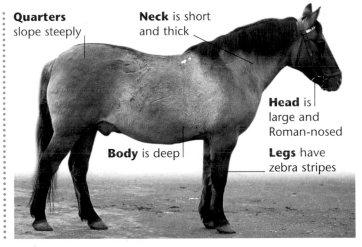

Quarters slope steeply

Neck is short and thick

Head is large and Roman-nosed

Body is deep

Legs have zebra stripes

Modern Tarpan

The new breed of Tarpan lives a natural life in herds on reserves owned by the Polish government. Despite its ancient ancestry, it is much less primitive-looking than Przewalski's Horse. Although its head is quite big and its neck is quite short, the Tarpan looks much more like a modern riding pony.

Although the original Tarpan is extinct, Professor Vetulani's new breed is so similar to the old one that some people think it still exists. Like Przewalski's Horse, it has a dorsal stripe and zebra stripes on its legs. The Tarpan's mane and tail are long.

Irish Draught

The Irish Draught was bred in its native Ireland as an all-around horse used for riding, driving, and farmwork. This breed dates back to the 1100s, and its ancestors include European heavy breeds and the Spanish Horse. It is large and strong and capable of carrying a lot of weight.

Natural jumper

This breed is a natural jumper. Both the purebred Irish Draught and the Thoroughbred cross are often used for foxhunting. They can clear all kinds of obstacles when ridden on cross-country courses.

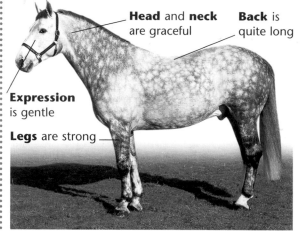

Head and **neck** are graceful

Back is quite long

Expression is gentle

Legs are strong

Despite its size—16 to 17hh (53–68 in.)— the Irish Draught is economical to keep. It has a calm temperament and is easy to ride and handle. It can be any solid color but is often gray. Although it is not very fast, this big horse is athletic and agile.

Hackney Horse

The Hackney Horse is an English breed that developed from two earlier breeds called the Norfolk Trotter and the Yorkshire Roadster. These were heavier, working horses, but the modern Hackney is more graceful because it was crossbred with Thoroughbreds. The Hackney is now a show harness horse that delights spectators with its fantastic action and appearance.

This lightly built and compact horse gives the impression of having great energy. It is high-spirited and moves very freely, throwing its forelegs well forward with each stride. Its action must be straight when seen from the front or the back.

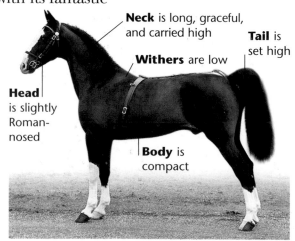

Neck is long, graceful, and carried high

Tail is set high

Withers are low

Head is slightly Roman-nosed

Body is compact

High-stepping horse

The Hackney's action, especially when trotting, is spectacular. It raises its knees and hocks very high and, as it moves, pauses slightly on each stride, giving the impression of an effortless, floating movement.

Cleveland Bay

This is the oldest of the native British breeds. It has been bred in northern England since the Middle Ages. Apart from Barb and Spanish crosses in the 1600s, the breed has been kept pure. These horses are strong, hardy, long-lived, and good-natured.

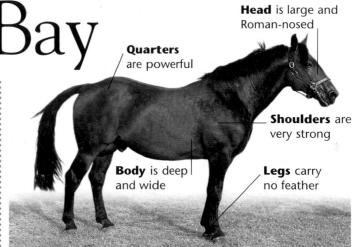

Head is large and Roman-nosed

Quarters are powerful

Shoulders are very strong

Body is deep and wide

Legs carry no feather

The Cleveland Bay is now classed as a rare breed. It is not used as a carriage horse so much anymore and is mainly used to cross with other breeds. As a result, the purebred Cleveland has almost disappeared.

Royal team

The Royal Mews at Buckingham Palace in London, England, has Cleveland Bays, which pull the royal carriages. The Duke of Edinburgh (left) is driving a four-in-hand team, which competes in cross-country driving events.

Key facts

- **Place of origin**
  North Yorkshire, England

- **Height**
  Around 16.2hh (66 in.)

- **Color**
  Always bay, with no white except a star

- **Uses**
  Driving, sometimes riding

Andalusian

The Andalusian horse, from southern Spain, is the modern equivalent of the ancient Spanish Horse, which influenced horse breeding worldwide. Most American breeds are descended from the Spanish Horse. The Andalucian is noble and proud, agile and athletic, with a good temperament.

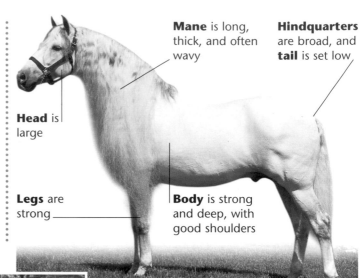

Mane is long, thick, and often wavy

Hindquarters are broad, and **tail** is set low

Head is large

Legs are strong

Body is strong and deep, with good shoulders

Ride and drive

Although it is mainly used for riding and is a popular dressage horse, the Andalusian is also driven. In its native Spain it is often used in harness during ceremonial and festive occasions.

The beautiful Andalusian horse stands between 15 and 16hh (59–64 in.). It is bay or gray in color, with the gray sometimes having a pinkish tone. The Andalusian carries itself proudly, is athletic, although not fast, and has a kind and friendly nature.

Lusitano

The Lusitano is similar to the Andalusian breed and is also descended from the Spanish Horse. It comes from Portugal and was used by the Portuguese cavalry and for light farmwork. This horse has spectacular high action, and it is taught "high school" movements. It is also used as a carriage horse.

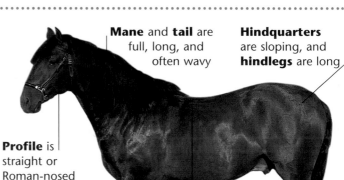

Mane and **tail** are full, long, and often wavy

Hindquarters are sloping, and **hindlegs** are long

Profile is straight or Roman-nosed

Cannon bones are long

Back is short, and **ribs** are well-rounded

Spanish walk

This horse is performing a special "high school" movement called the Spanish walk, which it has been trained to do. In this gait the forelegs are lifted up high and stretched out in front of the horse.

The Lusitano stands between 15 and 16hh (59–64 in.), and it can be any solid color. Gray is the most common color, but this horse may also be bay, dun, chestnut, or black. The Lusitano has a short, arched neck, sloping quarters, and a compact body.

Lipizzaner

The Lipizzaner is the horse used by the famous Spanish Riding School of Vienna, Austria. It is descended from the ancient Spanish breed, which is how the school got its name. The word "Lipizzaner" comes from Lipica, Slovenia, where these horses were originally bred.

From black to gray
Lipizzaner foals are born black, and their coats gradually get lighter in color as they grow older. They may be seven years old or even older before they turn gray.

Stocky horse

The Lipizzaner is stockily built, with short, strong legs. The shape of this horse's shoulders makes it suitable for use in harness, as well as for riding. Its action tends to be high, and its feet are strong. It is an extremely intelligent horse.

Spanish school

The Spanish Riding School trains Lipizzaner stallions to perform "high school" movements in an 18th-century arena lit by large chandeliers. It takes many years to train both the horses and their riders.

Key facts

- **Place of origin**
  Lipica, Slovenia

- **Height**
  15.1–16.2hh
  (60–66 in.)

- **Color**
  Usually gray but
  sometimes bay

- **Uses**
  General riding and
  as a carriage horse

- **Characteristics**
  Intelligent, docile,
  and long-lived

Levade
The levade is a classical "high school" movement. The horse rears up and balances on its hind legs.

Head
is often
Roman-nosed

Hindquarters
are powerful

Body is long and
withers low

Neck
is short
and thick

Legs are
powerful

Morgan

The Morgan comes from the eastern states of Massachusetts and Vermont. Morgans are descended from a stallion born in 1789, called Justin Morgan after its owner. This horse worked on the farm and raced, both in harness and under saddle.

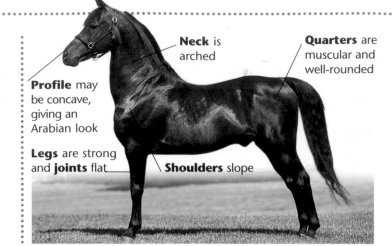

Neck is arched

Quarters are muscular and well-rounded

Profile may be concave, giving an Arabian look

Legs are strong and **joints** flat

Shoulders slope

Specially shod

Morgans are shown in either Park or Pleasure classes. Horses shown in Park classes have their feet trimmed and shod to produce a high action. If this is not done, the action is normal.

Standing between 14.2 and 15.2hh (57–61 in.), the Morgan is bay, brown, chestnut, or black in color. It is spirited, intelligent, and alert but has a good temperament and is easy to handle. Hardy, strong, and full of stamina, it is both ridden and driven.

Criollo

Descended from Spanish horses brought to South America in the 1500s, the Criollo is considered to be the toughest and soundest breed of horse in the world. The breed is native to the grassy plains of Argentina, where it is used by the gauchos, or cowboys, to work cattle. The Criollo is also found in Brazil, Uruguay, Chile, Peru, and Venezuela.

The Criollo can survive on little food in harsh climates. It is long-lived and has great stamina. In the 1920s Professor Aimé Tschiffely rode two Criollo ponies, called Mancha and Gato, from Buenos Aires, Argentina, to New York. The total distance was 9,920 mi. (16,000km).

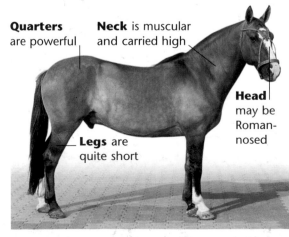

Quarters are powerful

Neck is muscular and carried high

Head may be Roman-nosed

Legs are quite short

Polo pony

Criollos are 14 to 15hh (55–59 in.) and are usually dun in color, with dark points and an eel stripe. They are often crossed with Thoroughbreds to produce the famous Argentinian polo ponies.

Quarter Horse

This first "all-American" horse was bred in Virginia in the 1600s for riding and farmwork. Its speed and agility made it perfect for working cattle. The breed got its name from English settlers who used to race these horses over quarter-mile (402m) tracks.

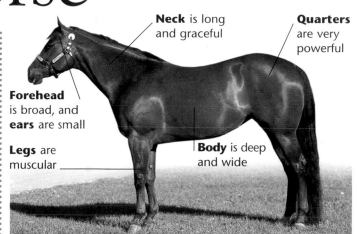

Neck is long and graceful

Quarters are very powerful

Forehead is broad, and **ears** are small

Body is deep and wide

Legs are muscular

Key facts

- **Place of origin**
  Virginia

- **Height**
  15–16hh (59–64 in.)

- **Color**
  Any solid color

- **Uses**
  Working cattle, showing

It has been claimed that the Quarter Horse is the most popular horse in the world, with over three million registered in the U.S. Agile and athletic, yet with a calm temperament, it is an ideal riding horse, as well as being superb at working cattle and performing in Western horse shows.

Sliding halt

A horse that works with cattle must be able to start, stop, and turn very quickly. In Western horse shows one of the most dramatic movements in reining classes is the sliding halt, where the horse stops instantly (right). Special shoes on the hind feet allow them to slide.

Pinto

The Pinto is a color type rather than a breed, although there are two Pinto breed registries in the United States. Descended from 16th-century Spanish horses, it has become popular in the U.S. Pintos can be black and white (piebald), chestnut, or brown and white (skewbald).

"Pinto" comes from the Spanish word *pintado*, which means "painted." There are two main color types: overo, which is mostly colored with white patches, and tobiano, which is mostly white with colored patches (rearing horse, far right). Pintos may vary in size and shape.

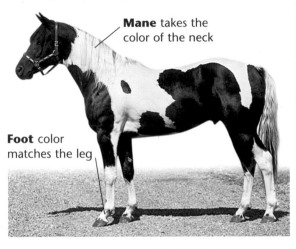

Mane takes the color of the neck

Foot color matches the leg

Native favorites

Pintos were favorites of the Native Americans because their coloring provided good camouflage. Today they are often bred for their color rather than their shape, and points are awarded for their markings at horse shows.

Palomino

This is another color type rather than a breed, so Palominos may be any size. The coat color should be as close as possible to that of a new gold coin, with a white mane and tail. Palominos were brought to the U.S. by the Spanish in the 1400s and 1500s.

Coat is golden

Mane and **tail** are white

White socks must not go above the hocks

Head may have small white markings

Palominos are bred by crossing palomino-colored horses with chestnuts or chestnuts with creams or albinos. In 15th-century Spain the palomino color was a favorite of the powerful Queen Isabella.

Barrel racing

Palominos may be any size or type and can be used for many activities, including showing and Western classes, as well as for general riding. This horse is negotiating a tight turn at a gallop as part of a barrel race in Tampa, Florida.

Appaloosa

This breed gets its name from the Palouse River in Washington. It was bred as a workhorse by the Nez Perce tribe of Native Americans in the 1700s from imported Spanish horses. Quarter Horses have been used to improve the breed, making it a strong, compact, and good-natured horse. It is agile and athletic, has great stamina, and is a good jumper.

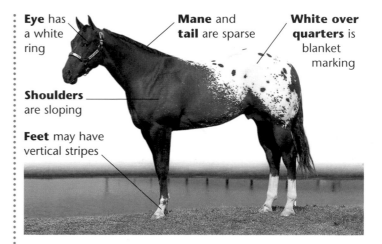

Eye has a white ring

Shoulders are sloping

Feet may have vertical stripes

Mane and **tail** are sparse

White over quarters is blanket marking

The main markings are leopard (white coat with dark spots—below); frost (dark background with white speckles); blanket (white quarters and loins, sometimes with dark spots); marble (roan, with a frost pattern in the center of the body and darker around the edges); and snowflake (dark background with white spots).

Key facts

- **Place of origin**
  Washington

- **Height**
  14.2–15.2hh (57–61 in.)

- **Color**
  White with dark markings

- **Uses**
  Riding, showing, jumping

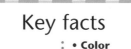

Tennessee Walking Horse

This breed was developed in the 1700s and 1800s by plantation, or estate, owners in the United States, who wanted a comfortable riding horse to carry them around their large areas of land. It is called a gaited horse because it can perform three extra gaits—the flat walk, the running walk, and the rocking-chair canter. All of these movements are smooth and comfortable for the rider.

The Tennessee Walking Horse is a popular riding horse for all ages in the U.S., as well as being a show horse. The breed stands 15 to 16hh (59–61 in.) and is usually brown, bay, chestnut, or black. It is said to be the most good-tempered of all horses.

Mane is clipped off at the top in the U.S.

Head is large

Shoulders are muscular

Legs are strong

Back is short

Tail is set high

American Saddlebred

The Saddlebred was bred in Kentucky in the 1800s. It is another gaited horse—three-gaited horses perform the walk, trot, and canter with high steps; five-gaited horses also perform the slow gait and the rack, both four-beat, lateral paces. The way the horse is shod accentuates its action.

The Saddlebred is usually bay, brown, or chestnut and stands 15 to 16hh (59–64 in.). It is mostly a show horse, but if it is shod normally, it can be used for harness or general riding.

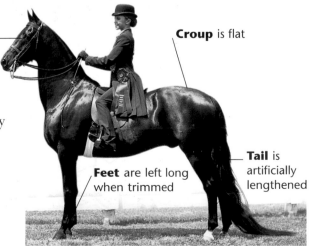

Head is carried very high

Croup is flat

Tail is artificially lengthened

Feet are left long when trimmed

Spectacular action

The rack (above) is a fast and spectacular pace in which each leg is raised high and lands separately. Special boots protect the front heels and pasterns from being injured by the horse's hind feet as they reach far forward.

Missouri Foxtrotter

This horse was bred in the 1800s in Arkansas and Missouri as a comfortable riding horse that could cover long distances quite quickly. The breed has a unique gait called a foxtrot, in which it appears to walk with its front legs and trot with its hind legs.

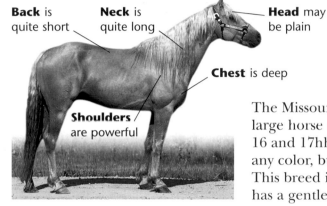

Back is quite short

Neck is quite long

Head may be plain

Chest is deep

Shoulders are powerful

The Missouri Foxtrotter is a large horse that stands between 16 and 17hh (64–68 in.). It may be any color, but most are chestnut. This breed is surefooted and has a gentle nature.

Comfortable ride

The Foxtrotter's gait is smooth and comfortable. It can travel at a speed of 5 mph (8km/h) for long distances and may go twice as fast over shorter distances. This breed is used for trail riding and showing.

Standardbred

The Standardbred is the fastest harness racing horse in the world. It was first bred in the U.S. in the 1800s. Most Standardbreds are descended from an English Thoroughbred that also had Norfolk Trotter ancestors. Standardbreds race either as trotters or pacers.

The Standardbred stands around 15.2hh (161 in.) and is usually bay, brown, or chestnut. More heavily built than the Thoroughbred, it is fast and has great stamina. This horse can cover one mile (1.6km) in one minute and 54 seconds.

Head and **neck** are carried high

Croup is higher than withers

Hindquarters are very powerful

Head is quite plain

Chest is deep

Legs are strong and sturdy

Mustang

The tough wild horses that once roamed the plains of the western U.S. are called Mustangs. They are descended from Spanish horses taken to the U.S. in the 1500s, which were turned loose or escaped and became wild. For centuries Mustangs lived a natural life. Today special efforts are made to protect the original type of wild horse.

Mustangs range in height from 13.2 to 15hh (53–59 in.) and may be any color. They are fast, strong, agile, and hardy. They do not always have good natures, but some are domesticated and used as riding and endurance horses.

Head may be Roman-nosed

Legs are strong and tough

Body is compact

In the wild

Mustangs were rounded up and used by cowboys for cattle herding. Some were tamed and ridden by Native Americans, and others were hunted. As a result, their numbers fell, but they are now protected by U.S. laws.

Waler

The oddly named Waler is Australian—its name comes from "New South Wales." It was bred from Basuto ponies, Arabians, Barbs, and Thoroughbreds to work on the huge Australian cattle and sheep ranches. It was a cavalry horse in the Boer War and in World War I. Now it is also used for police work.

Withers are high

Hindquarters are strong

Neck is long

Legs are strong, with plenty of bone

Body is deep through the girth

Riding horse

The Waler is sometimes called the Australian Stock Horse, but it is also an ideal horse for general riding. It is fast and agile and is a natural jumper. Some Walers perform in horse shows, doing displays of buckjumping.

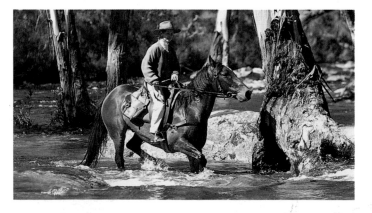

The Waler ranges in height from 14.2 to 16hh (57–64 in.) and may be any solid color. It is more powerfully built than the Thoroughbred. It is strong and tough, and its great powers of endurance mean that it can be ridden around ranches all day long.

Pony Breeds

Ponies are smaller than horses and have different features. They are deeper through the girth and have shorter legs. They often have feather on the lower legs and thick manes and tails. Ponies are surefooted and usually full of character.

Dartmoor

Small ponies have lived wild on Dartmoor, a large, rugged moor in Devon, England, for hundreds of years. Poor grazing and harsh conditions on the moors have produced strong, tough animals. Over the centuries Arabian, Thoroughbred, and Welsh Section A crosses have been used to improve this breed's quality.

Head is small and neat

Shoulders are sloping

Legs are strong

Feet are hard

Body is compact and well-formed

The Dartmoor is a first-class children's riding pony. It is strong enough to carry a heavy weight, has good paces, jumps well, and has a good temperament. It stands around 12.2hh (50 in.) and is bay or brown in color.

Wild on the moor

There are not many purebred ponies living wild on Dartmoor today. Most of them are bred in studs. The ponies roaming the moor look quite different. In the winter, to withstand the wind, rain, and snow of their native home, they grow very thick coats and long, shaggy manes and tails.

Exmoor

This pony is from the region of southwest England known as Exmoor. It is one of the oldest breeds in the world and dates back to the last Ice Age. Today it is classed as a rare breed. It stands only 12.2 to 12.3hh (50–51 in.) but is strong enough to carry an adult.

Eye is hooded, with a light ring around it called a "toad" eye

Muzzle is light-colored

The Exmoor is usually a mousy dun color, with light, mealy-colored areas around the eyes, muzzle, the inside of the legs, and the underside of the belly. The ponies may also be bay or brown.

Back is broad

Tail is wide at the top

Legs are short and strong

Head is small and neat

Hindquarters are strong and give speed and jumping ability

Shoulders are sloping

Legs are strong, with plenty of bone

Body is compact and deep through the girth

Connemara

The Connemara comes from the moors of western Ireland, where its ancestors have lived since the 1500s. Native ponies were crossed with Spanish, Barb, Arabian, Welsh Cob, and Thoroughbred horses to develop the breed. The result was a strong, sturdy riding pony, with good paces and jumping ability.

Connemaras can be gray, dun, bay, brown, black, chestnut, or roan. They stand 13 to 14.2hh (52–57 in.) and are hardy, docile, and intelligent. They are ridden by both children and adults and make good competition horses when crossed with Thoroughbreds.

New Forest

Since the A.D. 1000s ponies have lived in the New Forest in Hampshire, England. Over the years different breeds have been introduced, including Arabians and Barbs, so New Forest ponies have a mixture of ancestors. They are fast and have good, low action.

Quarters are strong and powerful

Neck is arched

Expression is alert

Legs and **feet** are strong

Shoulders are long and sloping

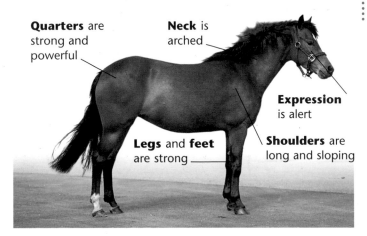

Forest pony

There are two types of ponies—one stands up to 13.1hh (53 in.) and the other 13.2 to 14.2hh (53–57 in.). Both are narrow in build, making them easy for children to ride. The ponies may be any solid color.

Most of the New Forest is scrubland. Local people, known as "Commoners," are allowed to keep ponies there. Many of these are in poor condition. The better examples of the breed usually come from stud farms.

Welsh Section A

The Welsh Section A, or Welsh Mountain Pony, has lived on the hills of Wales in Great Britain since pre-Roman times. It is thought to be the most beautiful pony breed. Strong and tough, with great powers of endurance, it is used for riding and driving.

Section A ponies should not stand taller than 12hh (48 in.). They look like miniature Arabians and are strong for their size. They may be any solid color, are surefooted and intelligent, and make good riding ponies.

Head is small and dished

Neck is long and graceful

Back is short and strong

Body is deep through the girth

Legs are sturdy

Welsh Section B

The Welsh Section B is also called the Welsh Pony. It was bred by crossing Section As with Section Ds and has Arabian ancestors as well. Originally the pony was used by farmers for transportation and for herding sheep that grazed on the Welsh hills. The modern type of this breed has existed since the early 1900s.

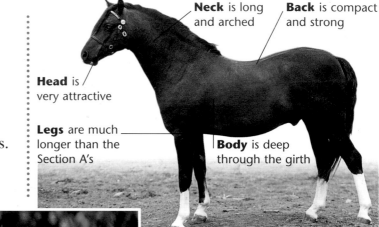

Neck is long and arched

Back is compact and strong

Head is very attractive

Legs are much longer than the Section A's

Body is deep through the girth

Section B ponies stand 12.2 to 13.2hh (50–53 in.) and may be any solid color. They have the character and gentle nature of the Section A but are more useful riding ponies because of their longer legs.

Competitive pony

As the Section B is taller than the Welsh Mountain Pony, it can be ridden by larger children and used in competitions such as gymkhana events. It has long, low action and is also a good jumper.

Welsh Section C

This pony was originally bred by crossing the Section A and Section D and is known as the Welsh Pony of Cob Type. Smaller than the Welsh Cob but stockier in build than the Welsh Pony, it was once used for all types of farmwork, as well as in the slate quarries of North Wales. Today it is often used for trekking and trail riding, as well as driving.

Neck is thick and carried high

Quarters are very muscular

Head is attractive

Shoulders are powerful

Legs are strong

This small pony should not stand taller than 13.2hh (53 in.). Despite its size, the Section C is very strong. It is also hardy enough to live outside all year long. It has a good temperament and may be any solid color.

Driving pony

With their fast action, Section C ponies are ideal for driving. They are also good riding ponies, can jump well, and are strong enough to carry light adults, as well as children.

Welsh Section D

The Section D, or Welsh Cob, was bred from the Welsh Mountain Pony, with crosses to Spanish horses, trotters, and Arabians between the 1000s and 1800s. The Cob was used for all-around farmwork and riding and for pulling carts in cities.

The Section D stands between 14.2 and 15.2hh (57–61 in.) and may be any solid color. It is famous for its fast, high-stepping trot, is an ideal driving pony, a good jumper, and is also used for riding and trekking.

Head looks like a pony's

Neck is strong and arched

Hindquarters are powerful

Legs carry some feather

Fell

This breed of pony is around 2,000 years old. Fell ponies come from Cumbria, England, and have Friesian ancestors. They were used as pack animals to carry lead from the mines to the docks and often traveled 240 mi. (386km) in one week. They were also ridden and driven and used for farmwork and herding.

These ponies are only 14hh (55 in.), but they can carry 220 lb.(100kg) packs or be ridden by adults. They are strong, hardy, surefooted, and energetic. They are always black or dark brown, with only small white markings allowed.

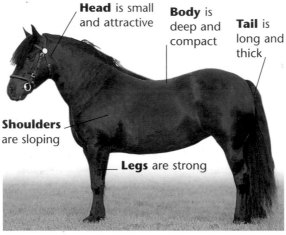

Head is small and attractive

Body is deep and compact

Tail is long and thick

Shoulders are sloping

Legs are strong

Good riding pony

The Fell's sloping shoulders make it more suitable for riding than the Dales pony, and it can be ridden by everyone in the family. It is also used for trekking. The Fell does well in harness and is popular for competition driving.

Dales

This strong and sturdy pony comes from Durham, North Yorkshire, and Northumberland, England. It was used as a pack pony to carry lead across the hills. The breed is around 2,000 years old and has Welsh Cob and Clydesdale ancestors.

The Dales is more of a harness pony than the Fell. It is taller, more solidly built, and has higher knee action. It stands around 14.2hh (57 in.) and is usually black in color. The Dales is also used for general riding.

Neck is thick and arched

Back is strong and muscular

Head looks like a pony's

Legs are short and strong and carry feather

Chest is broad and deep

Highland

The Highland has existed in Scotland since the last Ice Age and is the largest of Great Britain's pony breeds. They were bred for farmwork, forestry, and deer tracking, and there were three sizes—the smallest from the islands and the largest from the mainland. Today there is little difference between the three.

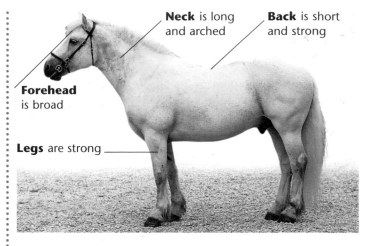

Neck is long and arched

Back is short and strong

Forehead is broad

Legs are strong

Powerfully built and very strong, the Highland looks like some of the ponies that are seen in ancient cave paintings. It often has an eel stripe along its back and zebra markings on its legs. Its shoulders are huge, and its feet are hard and tough. It is long-lived, easy to keep, and has a docile, gentle nature.

Key facts

- **Place of origin**
  Scottish Highlands, U.K.

- **Height**
  13–14.2hh (52–57 in.)

- **Color**
  Gray, dun, brown, black

- **Uses**
  Riding, trekking, harness

Champion pony
The champion Highland stallion Duart of Glenmuick (right) has the breed's characteristic full mane and tail.

Fjord

The Fjord is an ancient breed descended from Przewalski's Horse. It has many characteristics of primitive horses, being dun in color, with a dorsal stripe and sometimes zebra stripes on its legs. The Fjord is strong and surefooted, hardy, and economical to keep and has great powers of endurance.

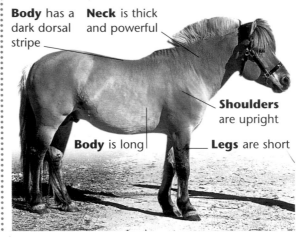

Body has a dark dorsal stripe

Neck is thick and powerful

Shoulders are upright

Body is long

Legs are short

The Vikings used ponies that looked like the Fjord and shipped them in longboats to Scotland and Iceland. Since ancient times this pony has been used for work on mountain farms, as well as being a riding and pack pony. This pony stands between 13 and 14.2hh (52–57 in.).

Special mane

The Fjord's mane is dark in the center and silvery white on the outside. It is cut to stand upright in a long curve, with the outer hair shorter than at the center.

Icelandic

Although the Icelandic is small, some people call it a horse. It stands between 12.3 and 13.2hh (51–53 in.) but is strong enough to carry an adult for long distances. The Vikings brought these ponies to Iceland, and the breed has been kept pure for 1,000 years. Icelandics are ridden, driven, and used for trekking.

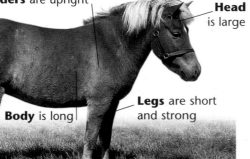

Quarters slope from the croup

Shoulders are upright

Head is large

Body is long

Legs are short and strong

As well as walking, trotting, cantering, and galloping, Icelandic ponies can perform a gait called the *skeid*, which is pacing, and the *tölt*, which is a fast, running walk. They take part in competitions for gaited horses.

Outdoor pony

Although the Icelandic winter is harsh, these ponies often live outside in a semiwild state. This makes them tough and hardy. They are also very surefooted, moving easily over the rough and mountainous ground of their island home.

Haflinger

These ponies have been bred in the Austrian mountains for over 200 years. All native Haflingers have a brand mark—a letter "H" and an edelweiss, the national flower of Austria. They were used for all types of farm and forestry work, as well as for riding. They are now popular trekking ponies.

Body is stocky and muscular

Neck is strong and thick

Legs and **feet** are very strong

As well as being sturdy and tough, Haflingers usually live for a long time. They start working at four years old and may continue until the age of 40—almost twice as long as the average horse. Haflingers have a docile temperament and are easy to handle.

Key facts

- **Place of origin**
  Austrian Tyrol

- **Height**
  13.1–14.2hh (53–57 in.)

- **Color**
  Chestnut or palomino

- **Uses**
  Riding, trekking, harness

Sleigh ride
Haflingers pull sleighs in the winter. Their harnesses may be decorated for Christmas.

New breeds of the U.S.

Some stallions produce foals that have similar characteristics to their sire, or father. This quality is called prepotency, and horses that have it may be used to start new breeds. Once a breed is established, a stud book is set up in which horses that meet the breed's standards are registered.

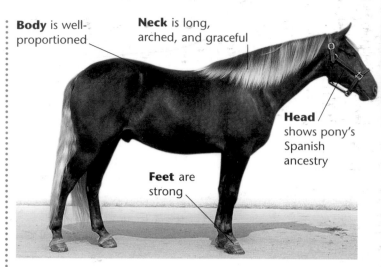

Body is well-proportioned

Neck is long, arched, and graceful

Head shows pony's Spanish ancestry

Feet are strong

Rocky Mountain

This pony may be the world's most recent breed—it was registered in the stud book in 1986. Although there are other colors, the favorite is a unique chocolate brown, with a flaxen mane and tail. The Rocky Mountain is sometimes called a horse because of its height. It is hardy and can survive in harsh winter weather.

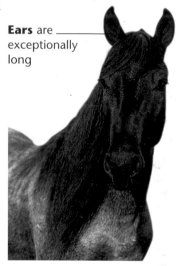

Ears are exceptionally long

Show driving
An American Shetland driving a show carriage is a popular attraction in the U.S. This pony also races in harness, and some types are ridden and jumped in the showring.

American Shetland

This pony is very different from the Shetland of the British Isles. The breed was developed in the 1880s by crossing lightly built Shetlands with Hackney ponies, and the result was a Hackney-type show harness pony.

Head is more like a horse's than a pony's

Head and **neck carriage** are like those of the Hackney Pony

Mane and **tail** are long and thick

Body is long and narrow

An American Shetland stretching out its legs in a showing pose

Special gait
Although this graceful animal is cantering, the characteristic action of the Rocky Mountain is a natural ambling four-beat gait. The Rocky Mountain can reach speeds of up to 20 mph.

Key facts

Rocky Mountain

- **Height**
  14.2–15hh (57–59 in.)

- **Color**
  Chocolate, with flaxen mane and tail, plus others

American Shetland

- **Height**
  Up to 11.2hh (46 in.)

- **Color**
  Any solid color

Pony of the Americas

- **Height**
  11.2–13hh (46–52 in.)

- **Color**
  Markings are the same as the Appaloosa

Pony of the Americas

This breed was started in Iowa in the 1950s when a Shetland was crossed with an Appaloosa. The foal that they produced was the first of the breed. Ponies of the Americas are small and stocky and have traditional Appaloosa markings. These ponies are docile and good-natured.

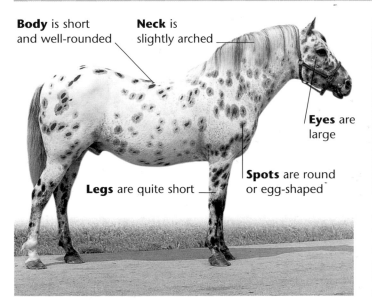

Body is short and well-rounded

Neck is slightly arched

Eyes are large

Spots are round or egg-shaped

Legs are quite short

On the leading rein
These ponies are small and easy to handle, so they are good for children who are learning to ride. First lessons are often on a leading rein.

Caspian

The Caspian is possibly the oldest breed of horse or pony that exists, and it may be the ancestor of the Arabian. Since prehistoric times it has lived near the southern coast of the Caspian Sea in what is now Iran. In the mid-1900s the breed was rediscovered, and these ponies are now bred in Europe, North America, Australia, and New Zealand.

The Caspian looks more like a miniature horse than a pony. It is lightly built, has a fine, silky coat, mane, and tail, and is very fast for its size. The Caspian stands 10 to 12hh (40–48 in.), and it is usually bay or chestnut in color.

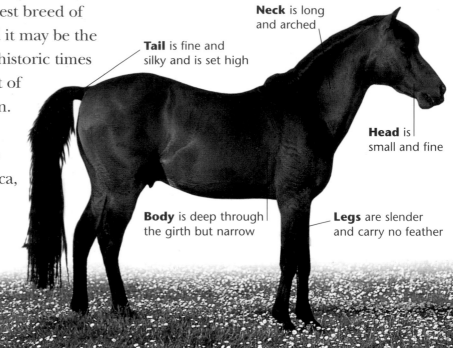

Neck is long and arched

Tail is fine and silky and is set high

Head is small and fine

Body is deep through the girth but narrow

Legs are slender and carry no feather

Chincoteague and Assateague

Chincoteague and Assateague are islands off the coast of Virginia, where these small wild ponies have lived since the 1500s. They may be the descendants of Barb horses that were once shipwrecked there.

Quarters slope sharply from the croup

Back is short

Head may be large and plain

These ponies have lived on islands for hundreds of years so they have not been crossed with other breeds. They stand around 12hh (148 in.) and may be any color. They are often skewbald or piebald (see Pinto on page 52).

Island ponies

Once a year the Assateague ponies are taken across to Chincoteague island, where the young animals are sold. These ponies are strong-willed and may be difficult to handle, but some are used for riding.

Basuto

This pony is named after the area of South Africa where it was developed between the 1600s and 1800s. It has Arabian, Barb, and Thoroughbred ancestors. The Basuto often had to endure harsh conditions, so this breed is strong and tough. The British used Basuto ponies during the Boer War.

The Basuto stands around 14.2hh (57 in.). It has great stamina and can be ridden every day for many miles. This makes the Basuto a popular trekking pony. It is usually brown, bay, chestnut, or gray in color.

Head may have Arabian features

Neck is thin

Back is long

Shoulders are upright

Feet are hard

Herding pony

Farmers in Lesotho, South Africa, use Basuto ponies for herding animals, as well as for riding around their land. In the past these ponies have been raced and were also used by the army and for polo. They are popular general riding ponies in southern Africa.

Boer

The Boer pony developed in the 1800s in South Africa and has similar ancestors to the Basuto. Most Boer ponies did not have to endure such harsh conditions as the Basuto, so this breed is often taller and of better quality. The Boer is known as the "Boerperd" in its native country. It is found in the northeastern part of South Africa, where it is used as an all-around farm horse.

Neck is long and carried high

Expression is alert

Pasterns are long and sloping

Body is narrow

Legs are long and slender

The Boer's height ranges from 13.3 to 15.3hh (55–62 in.), and it may be any solid color, including palomino. Some Boers are five-gaited and can perform the slow gait and rack, as well as the walk, trot, and canter. They are popular endurance horses.

Australian

Ponies were first brought to Australia in the early 1800s, and in the 1900s the Australian pony officially became a breed. Its ancestors include the Hackney Pony, the Shetland, the Arabian, the Thoroughbred, and the Welsh Mountain Pony (Section A), which it closely resembles.

The Australian pony stands between 12 and 14hh (48–55 in.) and is an attractive animal. Its action is free and level, and it is good-natured and easy to handle. This breed may be any solid color, and in Australia it is a popular riding and show pony.

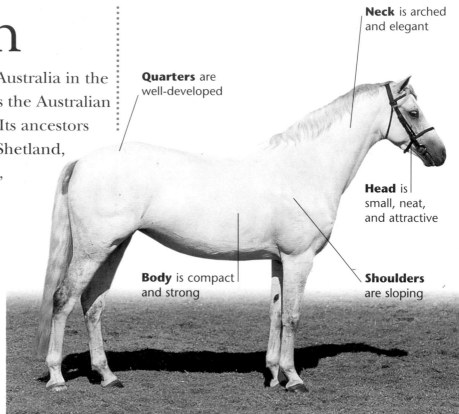

Neck is arched and elegant

Quarters are well-developed

Head is small, neat, and attractive

Body is compact and strong

Shoulders are sloping

Tiny foal

Falabella foals stand only around 4hh (16 in.), but they grow quickly. When the mother is pregnant, she carries her foal for 13 months, which is two months longer than other horses and ponies.

Falabella

The little Falabella is named after the family who created it near Buenos Aires, Argentina, in the early 1900s. They crossed tiny Shetland ponies with a small Thoroughbred and kept breeding using the smallest ponies produced. Falabellas are inbred, so they are not strong and need a lot of care and attention. They are not ridden, although they are sometimes driven. Falabellas are mostly kept as pets.

Tail is set low

Legs are not very strong

Body is deep

Mane and **tail** are thick

Head is large

Falabellas stand around 7 to 8.2hh (28–34 in.) and may be any color. People think of them as miniature horses rather than small ponies because they have fine bones and slender legs. They are clever and friendly and make good pets.

Shetland

The Shetland is the smallest of Great Britain's mountain and moorland ponies. It has lived in the bleak Shetland Islands, northeast of Scotland, for around 10,000 years. The harsh climate and poor grazing have made it very hardy. For its size the Shetland is probably the strongest of all horses and ponies.

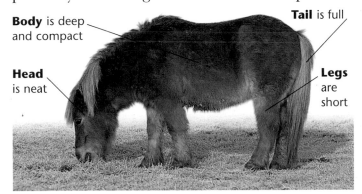

Body is deep and compact

Head is neat

Tail is full

Legs are short

Shetlands are measured in inches, not in hands, and are up to 42 in. (107cm) high. They can be any color. They are used as children's riding ponies and in harness, where they are especially good at scurry driving.

Tough ponies

These ponies can survive in the snow and strong winds of their island home. They grow thick coats and can live on very little food. Their small size means they can find shelter more easily than larger ponies.

Hackney Pony

The Hackney Pony is a smaller, ponylike version of the Hackney Horse. It was produced in the 1800s from Fell and Welsh ponies and the Yorkshire Trotter. These early ponies were very hardy, and today's Hackneys are strong and tough, with great stamina. Hackneys have a high neck carriage, short, compact bodies, and long, powerful legs. They can be 12.2 to 14hh (50–55 in.) and are brown, bay, or black.

Spectacular action

The Hackney's high-stepping action is a spectacular sight and produces much applause in the showring. Around 100 years ago these ponies could be seen on city streets, where they were used by tradesmen delivering goods. Today they are almost always show harness ponies.

Keeping
a pony

K eeping and caring for a pony is a
serious commitment. It is hard work
and takes up much of your time. It
is also exciting, rewarding—and a lot of fun!

Providing company

Horses and ponies are herd animals and do not like being on their own. Ideally they should live with other horses and ponies, but if this is not possible, then the company of other animals can be substituted instead. If you have to keep a pony on its own, visit it frequently and make it feel a part of family life.

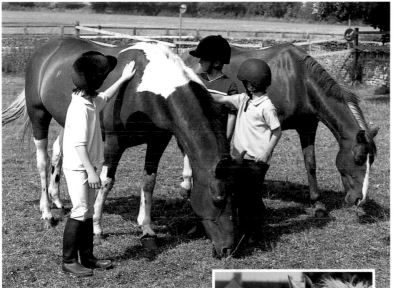

Human contact

Ponies like human company and will always appreciate your visits, though you may not be important enough to them to stop them from grazing! Be careful they do not tread on your feet as they walk forward. If you do offer treats, make sure there are enough to go around to all of the ponies in the group.

Ponies always enjoy a treat, but don't feed your pony treats every time you visit it because it will learn to expect them and might nip you.

Animal companionship

Once they get to know each other and realize they are part of a group that lives together, most animals become friends. Horses and ponies get on well with a variety of animals, from cats and dogs to livestock.

Although one horse or pony in a group is always dominant, two horses kept together usually become firm friends.

Horses and cats may enjoy each other's company, both in the stable or out in the pasture.

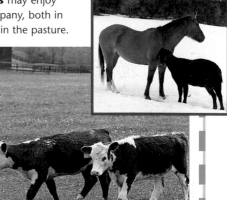

A friendly goat is good company for a lonely horse or pony, as are farm animals such as cattle and sheep.

Regular exercise

If a pony is kept in a stable, it has to be exercised every day. If it is not possible to ride it, then the pony should be turned out in a paddock for a while or lunged. Exercise keeps a pony healthy. Its circulation, heart, and lungs function better, and the bones and muscles are kept strong and healthy.

What a pony needs

A pony needs food and water, shelter from the weather, regular exercise, and companionship. In its natural state all these things are part of the life that it leads. But when we domesticate horses and ponies and make them work for us, they depend on us to fulfill all these needs. We owe it to them to do this as well as we possibly can.

Some form of shelter

A pony that lives in a pasture needs some kind of shelter from the sun and flies in the summer, and rain, wind, and snow in the winter. Trees and thick hedges provide a certain amount of protection, but a shelter built specifically for horses is the best solution, if it is possible.

Grazing in a pasture

Every pony should have access to good grazing for a part of each day. This is its natural way of life. Even if the grass is poor or during the winter, being out in the pasture allows your pony the freedom to move from place to place, roll, and occasionally gallop around, which helps keep it calm.

A suitable barn

If the pony is to be kept in a barn, or stabled, the building must meet certain requirements. The doorway should be high enough so the pony cannot bang its head. The stall should be well lit, with plenty of ventilation. It must have good drainage so that the bedding stays as dry as possible.

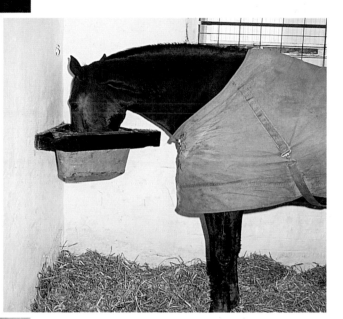

Feeding routine

A stabled pony needs regular feeding. The amount of food it needs depends on its individual needs and the amount of work it is being asked to do, but all stabled ponies need hay to replace the grass they would eat if they lived out in a pasture and grazed.

Bedding

The purpose of bedding is to provide a warm, dry, comfortable floor covering on which a horse or pony can lie down without knocking or injuring itself. It also takes some of the strain off the legs when a horse has to stand for long periods on a hard surface. Many different kinds are available. Whatever kind you choose, it should be at least 6 inches deep.

Straw is the dried stalks of wheat, barley, or oats. It is cheap to buy, but some ponies like eating it, and it can give them colic.

Hemp bedding is sold in vacuum-packed bales. It is useful for horses and ponies that have dust allergies, although it is expensive to buy.

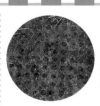

Rubber matting is very expensive, but saves time on mucking out. You need to use some bedding on top of it to soak up any wetness.

Wood shavings are sold vacuum-packed. Any dust is extracted, so they are good for horses and ponies with breathing problems.

Shredded paper is cheap, but some ponies are allergic to the ink in it. It is heavy to lift and unpleasant to handle when it is wet.

Far to walk
You may have to carry a pasture-kept pony's tack some distance.

Ways to keep a pony

You can keep a pony out in a pasture, in a stable, or a combination of both. Looking after a stabled pony is hard work and takes up a lot of time. It also costs more than keeping a pony in a pasture, but it is very convenient. A pasture-kept pony requires less looking after, but preparing it for riding takes longer. Many people think the ideal system is to put ponies in a barn at night in the winter and during the day in the summer, and let them live outdoors the rest of the time.

Winter pasture

In the winter, pastures can become very muddy, and your pony may be wet and dirty most of the time. This is bad for its feet and legs. But pasture-kept ponies are less likely to suffer from coughs and breathing problems than stabled ponies.

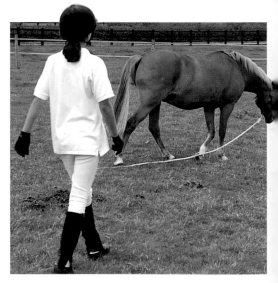

Catching a pony

Some ponies are difficult to catch, and some may try to pull away once caught. A trailing rope can be dangerous, so try not to let it go. It may be better to lead a difficult pony in a bridle.

Preparing for a ride

It is easy to prepare a stabled pony for riding. But before you can ride a pasture-kept pony you must walk to the pasture, catch it, and then get it clean enough to tack up.

Regular feeding routine

When ponies are stabled, they need feeding at regular times. Whether or not they have concentrated feed (page 99), they need hay several times a day, either loose or in a haynet, to give them the bulk food that grazing would provide if they lived outdoors.

Mucking out

When a pony is stabled, you have to muck out the stall thoroughly at least once a day, as well as removing droppings at regular intervals. This takes time, and it can be very hard work.

A stabled pony is entirely dependent on you for food and water.

Removing mud and stains

A stabled pony needs just a quick brush over before and after exercise to make it look presentable. With a pasture-kept pony, you have to remove all the mud stuck to its coat. It is especially important to remove mud where the tack fits, or it may rub and cause sores.

Carrying water to the pasture

If the pasture does not have a trough that fills automatically, you will have to carry fresh water to it every day. In warm weather, and if there are several ponies in the pasture, this can mean many trips back and forth with buckets.

Stables

A long barn that is divided into box stalls with a central aisle is called an American barn. It is convenient in bad weather, but there can be problems with ventilation.

Where to keep a pony

If you are a new owner, it is a good idea to keep your pony at a boarding barn where you will have knowledgeable people to help you. Types of barns and their fees vary. Some boarding barns charge less if they can use your pony for lessons. You may be able to rent a pasture and stall from a farmer, or be lucky enough to keep your pony in your backyard.

British stables

Typically in the U.K., each stall opens onto a central courtyard called the yard, which lets the horses see what is going on. An overhanging roof gives the horses (and people) some protection from sun and rain.

Planning a conversion

You may have a garage or outbuilding at home that can be turned into a barn. In most areas your parents will have to apply with local zoning boards for permission to keep "livestock." They will have to submit plans to the board. This process can take a long time.

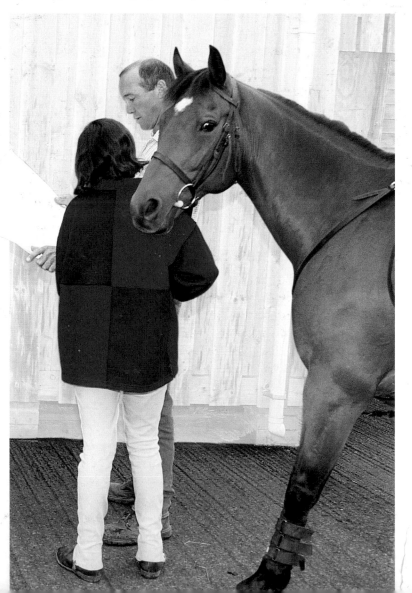

A pasture and pasture shelter

If you only have a pasture in which to keep
your pony, try to make sure there is some kind of
shelter. This will protect your pony from the weather,
as well as giving you a place where you can put your
belongings, groom the pony, tack it up, and feed it in
the winter. Remember not to leave tack in the shelter.

A farmer's pasture

A local farmer may let you rent a pasture and
possibly a stall too, although many do not like
having horses on their land. If you do find one
who is willing, it can be very useful because he
will probably be able to supply you with hay
and may even let you ride in his pasture.

A barn of your own

If you want to keep a pony in your own barn at home, you need to plan well beforehand. The barn does not have to be perfect or even conventional, but it must meet certain basic requirements and be safe and comfortable for the pony.

A converted building

You may be lucky enough to have a building at home that you can use as a stable. It must be in good condition with a weatherproof roof and a safe floor. It must also be well ventilated.

A ready-made stable

You can buy a wooden stable as a kit and have it assembled at your home. You will need some kind of level, solid base on which to stand it. This will probably mean laying a concrete slab. You need to consider the site you will use carefully before you go ahead.

Planning a barn

If you are considering keeping a pony at home, remember you will need more than just a building in which to house it. Although you may only be planning to use one stall, you will have to find space for storing feed, hay, and bedding, and the latter two take up a lot of room. You must reserve a corner not too near the building for the manure pile. Tack and blankets have to be kept somewhere, and if you do not have a paddock, you will have to find a pasture for a daily turnout.

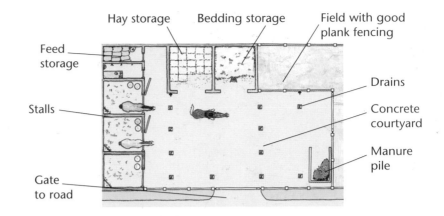

Feed storage · Hay storage · Bedding storage · Field with good plank fencing · Stalls · Drains · Concrete courtyard · Manure pile · Gate to road

A stable's requirements

When you are planning your stable, you need to make sure you have enough space. The stall has to be large enough—about 12 x 12 feet for a pony. The doorway and ceiling must be high enough for it not to bang its head if it tosses it up in the air. You will need a water supply nearby. Electricity is useful, but not absolutely essential. If you do have it, you must install light bulbs and switches where the pony cannot reach them.

Tying ring
It is useful to have tying rings both inside and outside the stall for tying up the pony and for hanging a haynet.

Automatic waterer
This needs to be plumbed in, but it will save a lot of time and effort carrying water buckets.

Manger
A pony or horse can drink and eat from a bowl or bucket put on the floor, but a manger is less likely to become dirty.

Good drainage
A concrete or brick floor that slopes gently to a drain will provide good stable drainage. A dirt floor can also be used.

Dutch doors
The open top half of the door allows the pony to look out. It should always be left open for ventilation.

Louvered windows
The top half of the windows should open inward to let in air but not rain, and the glass should be protected by grillwork.

Door bolts
Some ponies can undo the top bolts on their doors. A bolt with a lockable end prevents them from doing this.

Kick bolt
A foot-operated kick bolt on the lower part of the door saves having to bend down—which is useful when carrying things.

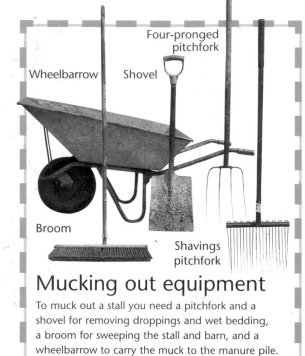

Wheelbarrow   Shovel   Four-pronged pitchfork

Broom

Shavings pitchfork

Mucking out equipment

To muck out a stall you need a pitchfork and a shovel for removing droppings and wet bedding, a broom for sweeping the stall and barn, and a wheelbarrow to carry the muck to the manure pile.

Stable management

Stable management means the organization and carrying out of all the tasks that are centered around the stable. A large part of stable management is the daily routine of mucking out, feeding, and watering, as well as keeping the building and its areas clean. Other jobs include the maintenance of equipment and checking feed and bedding storage areas.

Mucking out

A stall needs a thorough mucking out once a day—removing the droppings and wet bedding—and skipping out—just removing the droppings—several times a day. The process is much the same for straw or shavings. Some people use a deep litter system, in which only the droppings are removed daily and fresh bedding is added.

Clearing up
Sweep any remaining manure and wet bedding into a pile in the middle of the floor and use the shovel to put it all into the wheelbarrow. Continue sweeping until the floor is clean.

1 First remove all the obvious droppings on the surface with the shavings pitchfork and put them in the wheelbarrow.

2 When you have done this, toss the shavings to the sides of the stall, removing any droppings that fall out of them as you do so.

3 Once you have removed the top shavings, those still on the floor will be wet. Scoop them up with the shavings pitchfork.

4 Now the dry bedding is stacked around the sides and wet shavings have been removed. You can sweep the floor and shovel up the manure.

Bedding storage

Shavings and straw bales must be stored somewhere. Straw must be stacked under cover, preferably in a hay barn, where air can circulate around it and prevent it from becoming dusty or moldy. Shavings can be stacked outside, preferably under a waterproof cover.

A neat manure pile

Try to keep the manure pile neat. Ideally you should divide it into three sections: one that you are using to tip the manure on each day, one that you are leaving to rot down, and one that has already rotted down to be used as compost or disposed of elsewhere.

Clean water

Horses and ponies should have access to clean water at all times. Whenever you visit the stall, check the bucket to see if it needs more water. If the water is dirty, throw it away and rinse the bucket out well before refilling it. Every few days, scrub out the water bucket to keep it clean.

Water buckets are usually made of plastic or rubber.

5 If possible, leave the floor to dry and air for a while before pulling back the shavings to lay the bed. Bank up the shavings against the walls.

6 You may not always need to add new shavings, but when you do, open the bale carefully, cutting the tape with scissors or a special safety barn knife that has a recessed blade.

7 Shavings are very tightly packed in their bales. It is often easiest to use the four-pronged pitchfork to loosen them if you do not need to add a whole new bale to the bedding.

Choosing a pasture

A pasture suitable for grazing by horses and ponies should be level and well drained. It needs some form of shade and shelter (for example, trees, hedges, or a pasture shelter), secure and safe fencing, a clean water supply, safe access from the road, and a safely hung gate that can be locked if necessary. The pasture and hedges should not contain any poisonous plants.

Good fencing

Plank fencing is the best kind of fencing for horses and ponies, but some people use wooden post and rail *(above)*. Electric fencing works well if you keep it off the ground and check the supply regularly.

Good grazing

Horses and ponies thrive on a mixture of grasses, such as rye, timothy, and meadow fescue, with some beneficial herbs and weeds, such as dandelion, chicory, and yarrow. Be careful— do not let a hay-fed horse graze for long periods. Rich grasses may make it sick.

Poisonous plants

You should check any pasture in which you are going to keep a pony for poisonous plants. Any you find should be dug up and burned. If the pasture is near a garden, check that the pony cannot reach plants such as rhododendron, laburnum, oleander, and evergreen hedges. Most evergreens are poisonous.

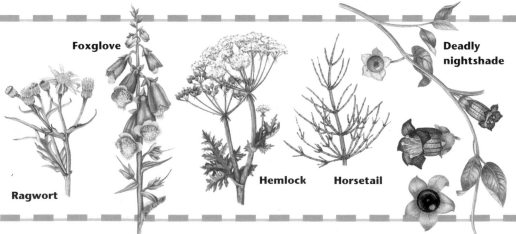

Foxglove

Deadly nightshade

Ragwort

Hemlock   Horsetail

Water supply

A stream is not ideal because it may be polluted. A water trough that fills automatically is very useful, or you may have to use buckets. Both the trough and the buckets need a good scrubbing regularly to remove the algae that builds up.

Secure locks
Unless the pasture is well supervised, keep the gate locked as a precaution against theft.

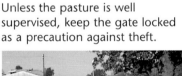

Safe gate

A correctly-hung and well-maintained gate that does not sag on its hinges, drag on the ground as you open and close it, or swing back and hit you as you go through ensures you can lead your pony into the pasture safely. The gate may be made of wood or metal.

Signs of a bad pasture

A pasture that is covered in droppings and has more weeds than grass, broken fencing, and a gate held in place with string is not suitable for a pony.

Uneven grazing
Clumps of coarse grass surrounded by bare pasture usually mean that the pasture has been overgrazed. It needs to be mowed and rested before being used again for horses or ponies.

Muddy pasture
A poorly-drained pasture with too many animals on it in the winter can quickly become badly cut up and muddy and is no use for grazing.

Too many droppings
A pasture covered in piles of droppings needs to be cleared and rested. The droppings kill the grass and contain many worm eggs. Grazing around these areas reinfests a horse.

Barbwire fencing
Barbwire should **never** be used for fencing where horses and ponies are kept. Many have been injured by it. The wire is especially dangerous if it is rusty or sagging.

Rhododendron

Yew

Laburnum

Bracken

Oak (acorns)

Laurel

Caring for a pasture

A pony's pasture needs a lot of attention to stay in good condition. Horses and ponies tend to graze in parts of a pasture until they are bare, leaving patches of coarse grass and weeds untouched. Putting other animals in the pasture evens out the grazing, but it may also need to be spread with fertilizer or lime and rolled in the spring if it gets churned up in the winter.

Pulling up ragwort

Ragwort is a tall, poisonous plant with small, yellow, daisylike flowers and ragged leaves. You should check a pony's paddock regularly for ragwort and pull or dig up any immediately. All traces of the plant should be destroyed. Put salt in the hole left after pulling it up to kill any remaining roots.

Removing droppings

Leaving droppings around not only damages the grass, but also encourages parasitic worms to breed. In a small pasture you should remove droppings every day with a shovel and a wheelbarrow or skip. This may not be practical if horses or ponies graze a large pasture, so the area should be dragged or harrowed instead to break up and scatter the droppings. The sun will then dry them out and kill off any worm eggs.

Pasture rotation

Grazing a pony paddock with sheep or cattle is one way to stop worm eggs developing because the worms can live only in horses' and ponies' digestive systems. If possible, a pasture should be grazed in rotation by horses, cattle, and sheep.

Mowing a pasture

Once or twice each summer a pasture needs to be mowed. A tractor pulls a machine that cuts down weeds, such as docks, nettles, and thistles, as well as the long, coarse grasses. This helps to stunt the weeds' growth and prevents them from scattering seeds. It also encourages new grass shoots to flourish, which provide more nourishing grazing.

Removing stones

Small stones can get lodged in a horse's or pony's hooves and cause lameness. Large stones can be dangerous if horses or ponies gallop around a pasture, causing them to stumble, sprain tendons, or even fall. It is a good idea to remove as many stones from your pony's pasture as you can.

Clearing trash

If a pasture is near a road, litter such as string *(left)* and plastic *(right)* may blow or be thrown into it. Plastic bags can kill a pony if eaten, and cans and glass bottles can cause severe cuts. String can become entangled around a horse's legs and also causes problems if eaten. You should check a pasture daily and remove any litter you find.

Turning out and catching

Turning out means putting a horse or pony out in a pasture. It is better to remove its halter to avoid any possibility of it getting tangled on fences or hedges, but leather halters, which break when caught on something, can be left on ponies that are difficult to catch. If your pony gets excited at the thought of joining its friends in the pasture, try to keep it calm.

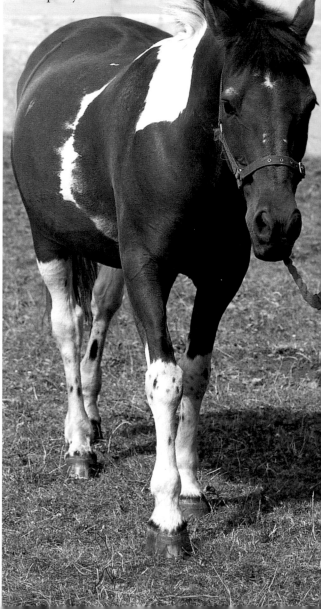

Carrots

Apple

Treats
Although too many treats can make a pony nip, giving it a treat when you visit it in the pasture can make it easier to catch.

Leading a pony

Ponies are usually led on the left-hand side. Hold the rope so that your right hand is near the pony's head with the palm facing down, and your left hand is near the end of the rope. Look straight ahead and walk level with the pony's shoulder.

Turning out a horse or pony

As you lead your pony toward the pasture other horses or ponies already there may gather around the gate. If this happens, ask a helper to open the gate for you and shoo the horses away quietly so that you can take the pony into the pasture safely.

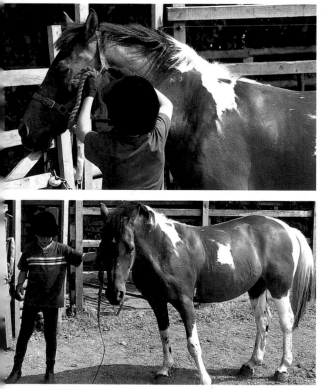

1 Lead the pony a few yards into the pasture after closing the gate behind you. Turn it around to face the gate, and undo the buckle on the halter.

2 Slip the halter off its head gently, and let it walk quietly away. If it gets excited and tries to whip around and gallop off, make sure you keep out of its way.

Keeping hold of a pony

If the pony misbehaves, bring your right hand down to the end of the rope near your left hand. Try your best not to let go, but bring the pony around you in a circle. Never wrap the rope around your hands. If the pony pulls away, it will drag you along.

Catching a horse or pony

Some horses and ponies are easier to catch than others. Approach a difficult horse with the halter behind your back and your hand outstretched holding a treat or a bucket with some feed in it. If the pony runs away, do not chase it. Wait for it to come to you.

1 Walk toward the horse's shoulder from the front, holding out a treat in your hand so that it can see it.

2 Give the pony the treat and quickly slip the lead rope around its neck before the pony has time to move away.

3 Put the halter over the horse's nose, still keeping the rope around its neck in case it decides to wander off.

4 Reach under its jaw with your right hand, and grab hold of the headpiece. Pass it over the top of the horse's head. Grab hold of the halter's cheekpiece with your other hand.

5 Buckle the headpiece so that it fits correctly— not too tight or too loose. Tuck the end of the strap through the buckle to keep it out of the way. You can then lead the horse in from the pasture.

Feeding a pony

A pony's natural food is grass. It has to eat a lot, but only a little at a time, to provide nourishment. When we replace grass with hay and other food, we must stick to this natural eating routine.

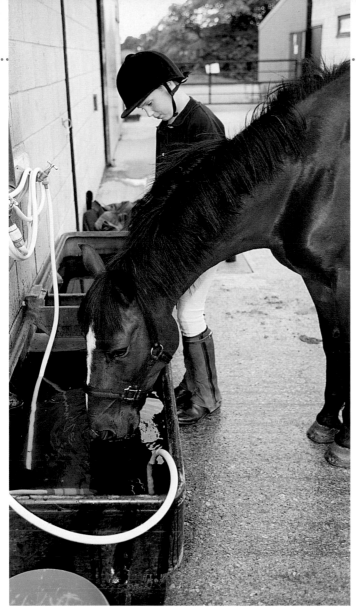

The rules of feeding

Horses' and ponies' stomachs are small, and their intestines are large. They need small quantities of food at a time, but a lot overall. This is how they eat bulk food such as grass or hay. But with concentrated feed (page 93), it is important that they do not get too much food in their stomachs at once.

Plenty of clean water

Clean water should always be available to a horse or pony. If it is not possible to allow it free access to water, then offer water at regular intervals before feeding. Watering after feeding can cause digestive problems, such as colic.

Feeding rules

Feed little and often, rather than giving large feeds.

Only feed fresh food.

Match the amount of food to the work the pony does.

Do not exercise a pony immediately after feeding.

Introduce new foods gradually to a pony's diet.

Feed plenty of bulk food, such as good grass hay.

Allow the pony to graze in a pasture for part of each day.

Feed a stabled pony something succulent, such as carrots or apples.

Feed at regular times each day of the week.

Keep the manger clean.

A haynet keeps hay off the floor.

Regular feeds

It is best to give a pony concentrated feed rations in several small feeds evenly spaced during the day. Work out a routine that you can manage, and stick to it. Ponies do not understand the difference between a weekday and a weekend—they expect their food to appear at the same time every day.

Different kinds of feed

Horse and pony feed can be divided into two main types. Bulk feed—grass and hay—forms the major part of the diet. A pony may manage on that alone. If it works hard, it may need up to 30 percent of its rations in the form of concentrated feed—also called hard feed.

Filling a haynet

Feeding hay on the floor is wasteful because the hay gets trampled and dirty. To fill a haynet, open it as wide as possible. Tear a slice of hay off the bale, pull it apart, and push it into the center of the haynet. You can get a rough idea of how much you are feeding by counting the number of slices you put in each time.

How much hay? To be sure exactly how much you are feeding, weigh the filled haynet.

Tying a quick-release knot

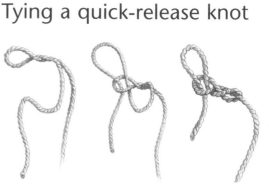

Make a loop in the rope and pull it through the tying ring. Twist the base of the loop several times.

Make a second loop in the loose end of the rope, and then push this through the first loop you have made.

Tighten the knot by pulling on the attached end of the rope. Undo the knot by pulling on the loose end.

Hanging a haynet

The haynet should be tied up high to prevent the horse from pawing at it and getting its foot stuck in it. Using a quick-release knot makes it easy to undo when it is empty.

1 Put the string of the haynet through the tying ring in the stall. Pull on the string to raise the haynet to the right height.

2 Loop the string through the rope mesh near the bottom of the haynet, and take it back up to the tying ring.

3 Put the end of the string through the tying ring again and tie the haynet firmly with a quick-release knot.

Types of concentrated feed

Oats can make ponies unmanageable so it may be better to feed barley instead. Most concentrated feed is best mixed with chopped hay and straw. Bran is used in mashes. Corn should be fed sparingly; sugar beet must be soaked in water before feeding. Pellets and sweet feed are easy to feed.

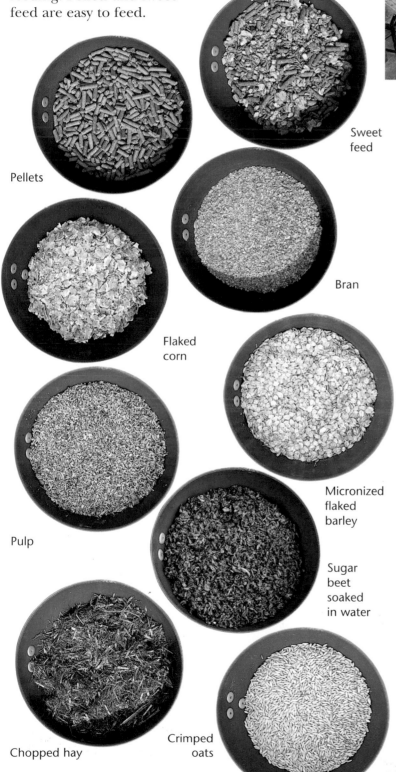

Pellets

Sweet feed

Flaked corn

Bran

Pulp

Micronized flaked barley

Sugar beet soaked in water

Chopped hay

Crimped oats

How to store feed

Feed must be kept in a cool, dry place and protected from rats and mice. In large stables sacks of concentrated feed are emptied into metal feed containers, but for one pony plastic garbage cans make good substitutes. Hay must be kept in a dry barn where air can circulate around it.

Supplements and treats

All horses and ponies need salt, which can be provided by a mineral block. In the winter feeding a little cod liver oil supplies essential vitamins. Ponies appreciate carrots both as treats and as winter feed. Apples are always very popular, but feeding too many can cause colic.

Mineral block
Ponies enjoy licking and gnawing at mineral blocks both out in the pasture and in their stalls.

Vegetable oils
Ponies need some fat in their diet, and this can be provided by oils such as vegetable oil. About one tablespoonful can be added to a feed.

A diet for your pony

Horses and ponies may be "good doers" or "bad doers." This means they can do well or even get fat on little food, or stay thin while eating a lot. An experienced horseperson will be able to work out a diet for a difficult horse or pony. With most ponies, it is better to be cautious about feeding, and if in doubt, give less rather than more. It is not healthy for a pony to be overweight.

Working out your pony's weight

You can check your pony's weight with a weight tape—a kind of tape measure. You pass the weight tape around the pony's girth, and as well as reading the measurement, you can also read off its weight. You may need an assistant on the other side of the pony to check that the tape is in the right position. You can also weigh the pony on a weighbridge.

Too thin or too fat?

Although they may both be the same height, a stockily built pony, such as a Highland, will carry much more weight than a thoroughbred type. So you have to assess a pony's fatness according to its type. It is important for the pony's health that it should be the right weight. A thin pony feels the cold. It uses its feed to keep warm, and it may have little energy left for working. A fat pony puts a strain on its joints and heart.

A thin pony
If you can see a pony's ribs, if its hip bones stick out, and its head looks too big for its neck, it is too thin. This may be the result of teeth problems, worms, or lack of food.

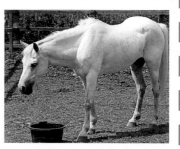

A fat pony
When you cannot feel a pony's ribs or spine, and it has thick pads of fat over its shoulders, and a large, round belly, it is too fat. Fat ponies are prone to illnesses such as laminitis (founder).

The perfect weight
A pony's outline should be smooth and rounded without any obvious fat. You should not be able to see its bones, but you should be able to feel them if you prod with a finger.

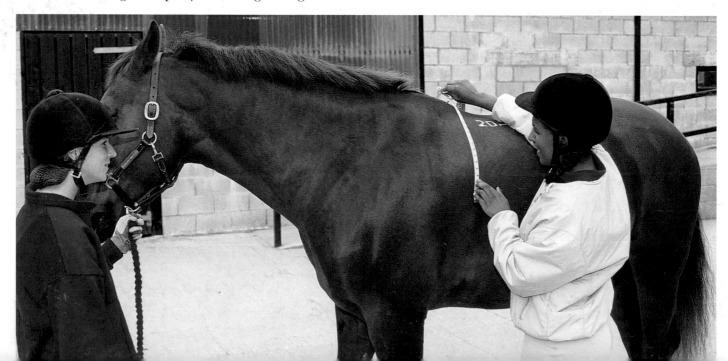

Measuring out

The only way you can be sure how much food your pony is eating is to measure it out. Work out how much food is needed by multiplying the pony's weight by 2.5 and dividing the result by 200. Decide how much of this should be concentrated feed and measure it out for each feed.

Starvation paddock

Lush summer grazing can be too rich for some ponies that become overweight and risk getting laminitis. Although it may sound cruel, they are best kept in an almost bare paddock, where they have to work hard to get grass to eat. An alternative is to stable them for most of the time and only let them out to graze for short periods.

Using a bucket muzzle

This is another way of stopping grazing ponies from eating too much. The muzzle has large holes at the front for breathing and small holes underneath that allow a certain amount of grazing and let the pony drink. The muzzle is held in place by a head strap, which you thread through the rings on the halter.

Soaking a haynet

Ponies that suffer from dust allergies and have breathing difficulties are best fed hay that has been soaked in a tub of water for a short while. A plastic garbage can is ideal. Filled haynets can be very heavy when wet, so be careful not to strain your back when lifting them out.

Weighing hay

It is a good idea to weigh filled haynets so that you know exactly how much hay the pony is being fed. You can buy special spring balances, which you can hang in the feed room or on a gate, designed to weigh a filled haynet. If you are feeding your pony soaked hay, weigh it before you soak it.

Grooming a pony

R egular grooming keeps a pony's coat clean and shiny. It is also a good way of checking it all over.

Grooming equipment

Grooming means cleaning the pony's coat, combing out its mane and tail, picking out its hooves, and keeping its eyes, nostrils, muzzle, and dock area clean. Each of these tasks needs a particular piece of equipment. Using the right equipment for each part of the grooming process enables you to carry out the work more efficiently.

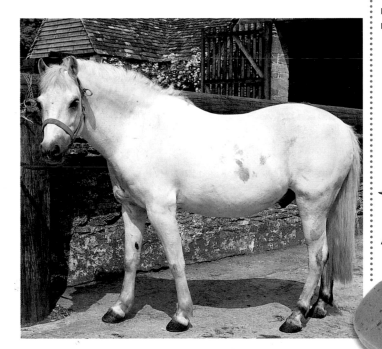

Why do I need to groom?

A healthy, hard-working pony needs grooming every day to keep its skin clean and in good condition. But all ponies need brushing over regularly to remove dried mud and stable stains and to keep the mane and tail neat. This not only makes them look better, but the ponies are also more pleasant to handle, and you and your clothes will stay cleaner.

Parts of the grooming kit

Ideally you need all the different grooming aids shown here, but you could start with a few and build up gradually. To begin with, a dandy brush, body brush, metal curry comb, hoof pick, and sponges are the most important things.

A dandy brush has stiff bristles and is used for removing dried mud.

A body brush has short bristles, designed to remove dirt and loose hair from the pony's coat and skin.

A plastic or rubber curry comb is used to remove mud and loosen matted dirt.

A metal curry comb is pulled across a body brush to clean it. It is not for use on the pony.

A hoof pick, which may have a brush attached, is used to remove dirt and stones from the hooves.

A water brush is used damp to lay the pony's mane and tail in place as a finishing touch.

A mane comb is mostly used when pulling the mane and tail to neaten them and separate the hairs before braiding.

Hoof oil is applied to the hooves with a brush to give a shiny finish for a special occasion.

One sponge is used to clean the eyes, nose, and muzzle; the other to clean the dock area.

A stable rubber or towel is used at the end of the grooming routine to remove any remaining traces of dust.

Grooming routines

A pasture-kept pony should only be brushed over lightly with a dandy brush to keep it neat. A hard-working, stabled pony needs to be groomed thoroughly each day to keep its skin in good condition. Both the dandy and body brushes are used in the direction of the hair of the pony's coat.

Clean the body brush on the metal curry comb after every three or four strokes.

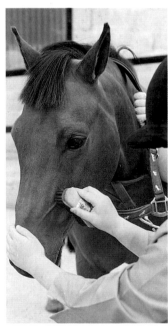

1 For a thorough grooming, first tie up the pony. Starting at the top of its neck on the left-hand side, groom it all over using the body brush.

2 Then undo the halter and rope. Fasten the halter around its neck while you brush its face gently with the body brush or a special face brush.

3 Standing to one side of the pony, hold out the tail. Release a few hairs at a time and brush them with the body brush. Undo any knots with your fingers.

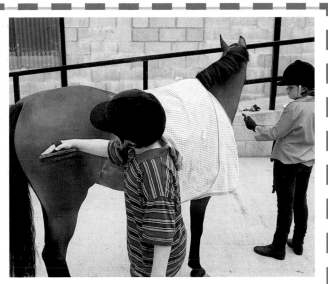

Sponging eyes, nose, and dock

The corners of a pony's eyes, the nostrils, the muzzle, if it is dirty, and the dock area under the tail should be cleaned every day with damp sponges. Use different sponges for the face and for the dock, and remember which is which!

1 Dampen the sponge, squeeze out the water, and wipe the corners of the eyes downward.

2 Rinse the sponge and use it to clean around the pony's mouth and inside its nostrils.

3 Using a different sponge, clean the dock, including the underside of the tail.

Quartering

Quartering means a quick brushing over of a horse or pony to remove stable stains and shavings or straw from the mane and tail. This will make it look neat before going out for exercise. The real work of grooming is done after exercise. In cold weather the blanket can be left over the forehand or quarters to keep the pony warm.

Fold back the blanket over the pony's quarters while grooming its forehand. Do both sides, then fold the blanket forward over its forehand so you can groom its quarters.

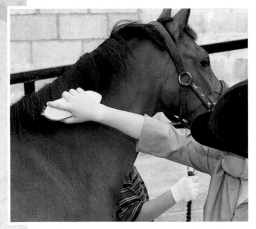

4 To clean the mane and remove any tangles, first brush it out thoroughly with the body brush. For a final, neat finish, dampen the water brush and use it to lay the mane in place.

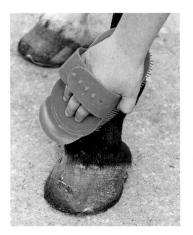

5 Although dried mud should be removed first, you can use a plastic or rubber curry comb instead of a dandy brush to remove any you may have missed on the legs.

6 The final step is to go all over the pony's body with a stable rubber. This is a cotton cloth that removes any remaining traces of dust and loose hairs and gives a glossy finish to the coat.

Hoof and foot care

Taking care of a horse's or pony's hooves is one of the most important tasks an owner must carry out. A pony's hooves must be sound. You should check and clean out a pony's hooves before and after riding, and on nonriding days, do it at least once. You must also have them regularly trimmed by a farrier and shod (pages 110–111) if you ride on rough tracks and roads.

When feet need attention

If a pony's hooves have not been trimmed regularly, the horn of the hoof will grow long and ragged and may split. When a pony does a lot of road work, the shoes will wear thin quickly and need renewing regularly. Overgrowth of the hooves makes the shoe nails come loose, and the shoe may come off.

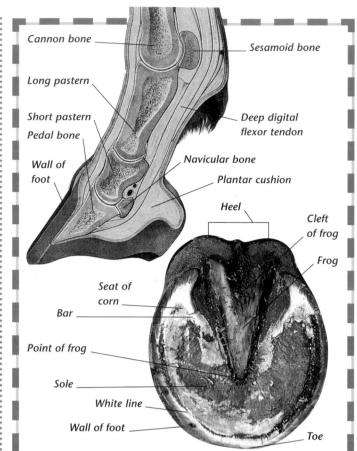

Cannon bone
Sesamoid bone
Long pastern
Short pastern
Deep digital flexor tendon
Pedal bone
Wall of foot
Navicular bone
Plantar cushion
Heel
Cleft of frog
Frog
Seat of corn
Bar
Point of frog
Sole
White line
Wall of foot
Toe

Structure of the foot

The outer casing of a horse's hoof is made of insensitive horn composed of leaves, or laminae. Deep within the foot are the bones, which are held in place by sensitive laminae—fleshy leaves—which interlock with the outer laminae. It is the sensitive laminae that become inflamed in laminitis. The sides of the hoof are called the wall, and underneath is the sole.

Overgrown hooves
If the hoof is allowed to become overgrown, the toes get too long and turn up, and the pony's weight goes back on its heels, altering the foot's balance. It can take a long time to correct this.

Raised clenches
When the hoof has been neglected and allowed to grow too long, the clenches (the ends of the nails that hold the shoe on) rise out of the hoof wall. The pony can injure itself on them and may lose the shoe.

Stones lodged in the hoof

Sometimes horses pick up small stones in their hooves, which lodge in the grooves on either side of the frog. If they get wedged in, they can damage the hoof, causing pain and lameness. You can remove them by digging them out with a hoof pick.

Picking up and cleaning out a hoof

Be positive in your actions when you pick up a pony's foot. Slide your hand firmly down each leg so that you do not tickle it. Always use a hoof pick from the heel of the foot to the toe, paying particular attention to the grooves between the frog and the bars and to the cleft of the frog itself.

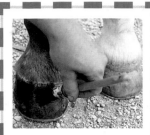

Oiling the hooves

Applying hoof oil to a horse's hooves makes them look shiny, but you should not do it too often or it can prevent the hoof from absorbing moisture. Pick out the hooves and scrub off any mud with a water brush before you start. Let the hooves dry, then apply the oil with a small brush. Hoof oil will not improve the quality of the hoof's horn. Only a special diet can do this.

1 When you want to pick up and examine a pony's hind hoof, start by putting your hand on the side of its hindquarters and sliding it down toward its leg.

2 Pass your hand firmly down the back of its hind leg. Do not be nervous when you are handling a pony or it will sense it and become nervous as well.

3 Continue down the back of its leg until you reach the hock. Keep your own feet away from the pony's in case it treads on you.

4 When you reach the pony's hock, bring your hand around to the front of its leg and move down over the cannon bone.

5 When you reach the fetlock joint, grasp it firmly and try to lift it, saying "Up" as you do so. Crouch—do not kneel—beside the pony.

6 Hold the pony's hoof in one hand while you use the hoof pick from the heel toward the toe in the other. A skip is useful for the dirt.

Washing a pony

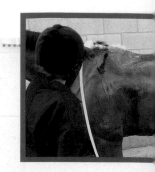

Only wash a horse or pony if it is absolutely necessary. Choose a warm, sunny, and windless day. Washing removes much of the oil from a horse's or pony's coat. This makes them look clean and shiny, but means that until the oil builds up again, they will feel the cold and have no protection against the rain. They may need to wear a blanket if the weather turns cooler.

Bucket of water

Shampoo

Sweat scraper

Sponge

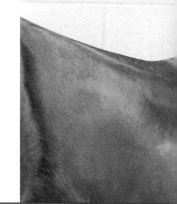

Equipment for washing
Before you start collect all the necessary equipment and put it where you can easily reach it.

Washing routine

It is important to keep the shampoo out of the pony's eyes, so when you are washing its neck and mane make sure its head is held up. Do not shampoo its face, just wipe it over with a clean, damp sponge.

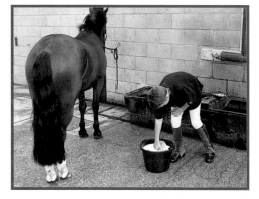

1 Tie up the pony where the water can drain away. Fill a bucket with warm water and mix in the shampoo.

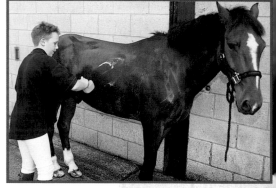

2 Dip the sponge in the water and rub it over the pony's coat in the direction of the hair. Cover the whole body, but not the head.

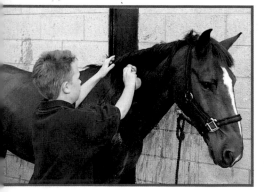

3 Wash the mane with the sponge, then rinse off all traces of the shampoo with another sponge and several buckets of water, or use a hose if the pony does not mind.

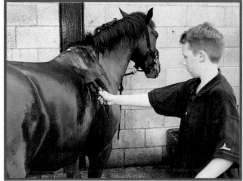

4 After rinsing use the sweat scraper to remove the excess water, pulling it across the pony's body following the lie of the coat. If you do not have a sweat scraper, you can use the side of your hand.

5 Gently comb out the wet mane. If there are knots and tangles in it, undo them carefully with your fingers before combing. Do not try to drag them out with the comb or you will pull out the hairs.

Rinsing the saddle patch

In warm weather when a horse returns from exercise with a sweaty saddle patch, you can hose it down—if this does not scare it— or sponge off the sweat.

1 Wash the top of the tail with a wet sponge, warm water, and shampoo, as you did the pony's body.

2 Rinse the tail in several buckets of clean water, swishing it around with your hand.

Washing a pony's tail

A pony's tail may need washing frequently, especially if it is a pale color. Doing so will not chill the pony. Use a bucket of warm water and shampoo, lifting up the bucket to get as much of the tail in it as possible. Hold up the bucket with one hand while you squeeze dirt out of the tail with the other.

6 Rub an old towel all over the pony in the direction of the hair to dry it off as much as possible. Squeeze out the water from its mane in the towel, and dry its neck underneath it. Do not forget to dry the pony's legs and heels as well.

7 On a hot day the pony will dry off naturally in the sun. If the sky clouds over, put an antisweat sheet or a cooler blanket over it, and walk the pony around until it is dry to prevent it from catching a chill.

Clipping a pony

Horses and ponies grow thick coats in the winter. If they are worked hard, they sweat a lot and become fatigued. To avoid this, the areas where they sweat the most have the hair clipped off. A clipped horse or pony needs a blanket to keep it warm when it is not working, even if it lives in a stable. Clippers must be handled with care, and the job is best done by an adult.

The hair is completely clipped off from the horse's head and neck.

Bandit clip
The horse is clipped all over except for its face, where the hair is left as protection from the rain. It is also a useful clip for a head-shy horse.

A bib clip runs in a straight line down the side of the neck.

Bib clip
The pony is clipped on the face and the front of the neck, chest, and shoulders. This clip is used for a horse or pony that sweats a lot on the neck.

Hunter clip
All the hair is clipped except for the saddle patch and the legs, which are left unclipped for protection against sores and thorns.

Belly clip
The hair is removed from the belly and up between the forelegs. A variation is to clip the hair on the underside of the neck too.

Different types of clips

The different styles of clips reflect the amount of work a horse or pony is expected to do. Some hard-working horses are fully clipped; others have areas of winter coat left on for protection against the weather, saddle sores, cuts, and thorns.

Trace clip
This is a popular clip for working ponies. Hair is removed from the underside of the neck, the belly, and the lower part of the body.

Clipping equipment

Clipping machines are usually electrically operated. They have a number of blades, from fine to coarse, depending on the type of hair to be cut. The blades need oiling and cleaning regularly when in use.

Main clippers

Small clippers

The blanket area keeps the horse warm and dry.

The coat is cut in a semicircle where the flank joins the quarters, following the line of the hair.

Blanket clip

This clip gets its name from the blanket area left unclipped on the back, which protects fine-coated horses against bad weather. The legs are also left unclipped. It is a useful clip for hard-working horses and is often used as an alternative to the hunter clip. With this clip, as with others, the areas to be left are marked out in chalk before clipping.

The clipping line at the top of the legs always slopes down from front to back.

The clippers are used with even pressure against the lie of the coat. They should move parallel to the skin without digging into it.

Blades for trimming coarse hair

Blades for trimming fine hair

Brush for cleaning clippers

Oils to lubricate clippers

Using the clippers

Clippers should always be used with a circuit-breaker to cut off the electricity if anything goes wrong. It is a good idea to wear rubber-soled shoes. The horse's coat must be clean and dry, and a haynet may help keep it quiet.

Choosing a blanket

When a horse or pony has been clipped, it needs to wear a blanket to make up for the loss of its winter coat and to keep it warm. On cold winter nights it may need more than one blanket or an extra sheet under the blanket. To be comfortable, the blanket should be long enough to cover the belly and should reach down to the root of the tail. Clipped horses are turned out in a turnout blanket to keep off the rain.

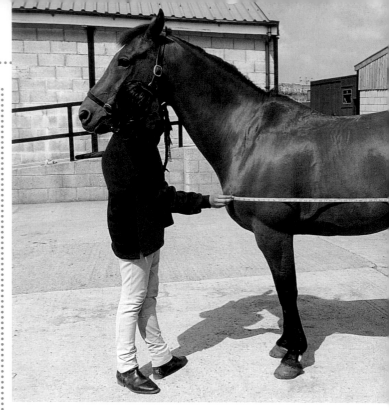

Measuring for a blanket

You need a long tape measure and an assistant to do this. Measure from the center of the horse's chest to the farthest point of its hindquarters. Blanket sizes go up in about 3 inch increments, so you have to buy the nearest size.

Types of blankets

Blankets are made in a variety of styles, shapes, and materials. The latter may be natural, such as cotton, wool, or canvas; or synthetic, usually nylon or polyester. All blankets fasten across the front of the chest with either one or two straps. They are then held in place either by a roller, which goes across the horse's back and around its belly like a girth, or by crossed surcingles. These are sewn onto the right-hand side of the blanket and pass under the horse's belly to fasten on the left side, crossing over from front to back. There are special kinds of blankets for specific purposes, although most horses and ponies just need a stable blanket and a New Zealand rug.

An antisweat sheet is a mesh blanket used on a sweating horse to prevent chills as it cools down.

A stable blanket keeps the horse warm indoors. It may be quilted or made of canvas.

A New Zealand rug is waterproof. It is used when the horse is out in the pasture in the winter.

A summer sheet is a cotton blanket used to keep the horse clean at shows and when traveling.

An exercise sheet is used to keep the horse's back warm during winter exercise.

A hooded New Zealand rug also keeps the pony's neck warm in bad winter weather.

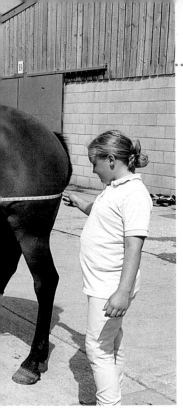

How to put on a blanket

When you put on a pony's blanket, do not fling it onto the pony's back—lower it gently. Put the blanket on forward of where it should lie, so you can slide it back into place, leaving the pony's coat lying flat.

Crossed surcingles

These should be adjusted by sliding the buckles so they fit comfortably around the pony's belly. They do not need to be tight—there should be room for your hand to fit between them and the pony.

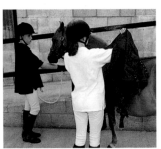

1 Tie up the pony. Carry the blanket folded in half with the back part folded forward over the front part.

2 Holding the blanket in both hands, lower it carefully onto the pony's back in front of where it should fit.

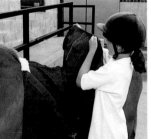

3 Unfold the back part of the blanket and lay it over the pony's quarters. Check that it is lying straight.

4 Fasten the breast straps, and then slide the blanket back until it lies in the correct position on the pony's back.

5 Undo the surcingles on the right side. Reach under the pony's belly for them from the left and fasten them.

6 Finally make sure that the blanket does not press down on the pony's withers and that it is not too tight across the pony's chest.

Roller

A blanket may be held in place with a roller, which fits tightly around the horse. An anticast roller has an arch in the center to prevent a horse from getting stuck, or cast, when it rolls.

Anticast roller

Leg straps

New Zealand rugs are held in place by leg straps, with one looped through the other to prevent them from rubbing. They must be attached correctly.

Taking off a blanket

Tie up the pony. If the blanket has a roller, undo it first and lift it off the pony's back. Make sure that the breast straps, surcingles, and any leg straps are unfastened before removing the rug.

1 When you have undone the surcingles, tie them loosely in place on the right-hand side.

2 Undo the breast straps. Fold the front of the blanket to lie over the back.

3 Holding the folded blanket with both hands, slide it back off the pony's quarters.

Other care routines

Taking care of a pony involves much more than housing, feeding, and grooming. Equipment must be kept clean and organized. Its hooves need to be trimmed and shod on a regular basis. It may have to travel, and in extreme weather conditions it may need special care.

Checking the legs
When you get back to the stable, check the pony's legs for small cuts or any thorns it may have picked up, and feel for any heat or swelling.

Walking home
When you are not on a busy road, loosen the girth by one hole, and let your pony walk on a loose rein to stretch its neck muscles.

At the end of a ride

Horses and ponies can get hot, sweaty, and excitable during a ride. Always walk your pony the last mile or two home to let it cool off and calm down. At the end of a hard day, dismount, run the stirrups up, loosen the girth, and lead it home.

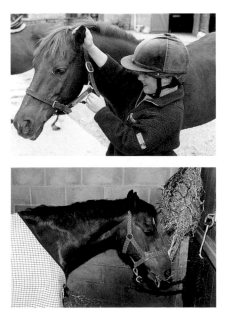

Rubbing the ears
A tired, wet horse may have cold ears. You can restore the circulation to the ears by grasping them at the base and pulling them gently through your cupped hands.

All blanketed up
If the pony is dry, brush off any mud before putting on its blanket. If it is wet, put straw under the blanket. Bandage wet and muddy legs over straw or cotton padding.

Care after exercise

On your return home unsaddle the pony, check it over, and clean its hooves. Brush off any mud or sweat marks. In hot weather you can sponge these off. Put on its blanket or an antisweat sheet, and if it is tired and thirsty, offer it half a bucket of lukewarm water. You can give it more later. Give a stabled pony a haynet before its feed. If it is pasture kept and it is not cold or sweating, you can turn it out.

Shoeing a pony

Ponies' and horses' hooves grow like your fingernails and need trimming every six to eight weeks to keep them in good condition. Shoeing prevents the hooves from wearing down too quickly when the pony is exercised on hard surfaces like roads. The person who trims and shoes a pony is called a farrier, or blacksmith. Most farriers have mobile forges and travel around to work at their clients' premises.

Hot shoeing

When a shoe is heated in a furnace before being tried on a pony's hoof, the process is called hot shoeing. Because the horn of the foot is insensitive, like your nails, the pony cannot feel it. A pony may need new shoes each time the farrier visits, but if the shoes are not very worn, the farrier will simply reshape them and use them again.

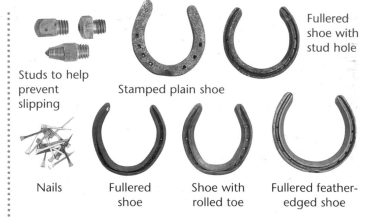

Studs to help prevent slipping

Stamped plain shoe

Fullered shoe with stud hole

Nails

Fullered shoe

Shoe with rolled toe

Fullered feather-edged shoe

Types of shoes

Most horses and ponies wear fullered shoes, which have a groove running around them for better grip in the mud. Farriers can make special types of shoes to correct most horses' and ponies' foot problems, as well as shoes for various kinds of work.

1 Using the buffer and mallet, the farrier cuts the nail ends, or clenches, that hold the shoe onto the foot.

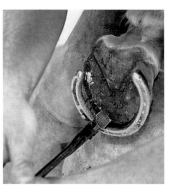

2 When he has cut the clenches, he levers off the shoe with pincers, starting at the heel and moving toward the toe.

3 He neatly cuts away the excess growth of the horn all the way around the hoof using the hoof cutters.

8 He then tries the shoe in place on the hoof. The heat burns the horn, causing it to smoke.

9 When he is satisfied, he cools the shoe in a bucket of water before starting to nail it onto the pony's hoof.

10 He hammers the nails through holes in the shoe to hold it in place, starting at the toe and working back.

Fitting studs

So that horses and ponies can be ridden in wet or muddy conditions, studs are sometimes screwed into special holes in the heels of their shoes.

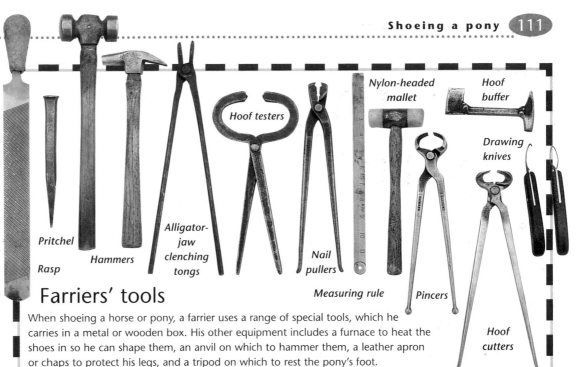

Pritchel

Rasp

Hammers

Alligator-jaw clenching tongs

Hoof testers

Nail pullers

Measuring rule

Nylon-headed mallet

Pincers

Hoof buffer

Drawing knives

Hoof cutters

Farriers' tools

When shoeing a horse or pony, a farrier uses a range of special tools, which he carries in a metal or wooden box. His other equipment includes a furnace to heat the shoes in so he can shape them, an anvil on which to hammer them, a leather apron or chaps to protect his legs, and a tripod on which to rest the pony's foot.

4 He evens out the wall of the hoof, sole, and frog, cutting off any ragged bits with a drawing knife.

5 Using the rasp, he makes sure that the weight-bearing surface of the hoof is absolutely smooth and level.

6 He then heats the shoe in an oven called a furnace until it is red-hot, handling it carefully with pincers.

7 He hammers the hot shoe into shape on the anvil, still holding it with the pincers and reheating it if necessary.

11 The nails come out of the side of the hoof and the farrier twists off their ends with the claw of a hammer.

12 Resting the shoe on the pincers, he hammers down the projecting nail ends to form the clenches.

13 With the foot on a tripod, he uses the rasp to smooth the ends of the clenches and the rim of the hoof wall.

14 The finished hoof should look neat and even, with six or more nails holding the new shoe in place.

Traveling safely

If you want to take part in riding club events, shows, or gymkhanas you will need to transport your pony in a van or a trailer. Once they get used to it, most horses and ponies do not mind this and learn to brace themselves against the movement of the vehicle. In doing so, however, they may knock their legs, so they need to wear protective gear. They also wear blankets to keep them warm and clean.

Storage
Water can be carried in a large plastic container.

Providing food and water

While traveling, a haynet will keep your pony happy. Store hay for your return trip inside the trailer rather than hanging it outside where it may be contaminated by exhaust fumes. On a long journey you may also need to take water.

Travel boots
Shaped and padded travel boots fit around the lower part of the pony's legs and are held in place by several Velcro straps.

Boots and bandages

To protect a horse's or pony's legs you can either use special travel boots or bandages. Travel boots cover the legs from the knee or hock to the coronet at the top of the hoof (pages 14–15). If bandages are used, the horse or pony may also need to wear kneecaps and hock boots to cover its joints.

Travel bandages
Used over felt padding, these are put on in the same way as first-aid bandages (pages 120–121).

1 Start by laying the bandage across the top of the pony's tail, leaving the end sticking up.

2 Then take the bandage under the tail and bring it around to the top, holding the end.

3 After a couple of turns of bandage around the tail, fold down the end you left out.

Bandaging a pony's tail

The top part of a pony's tail is bandaged before traveling to stop the pony from rubbing it against the back of the trailer. This also lays the hairs flat and keeps the tail neat. The bandage needs to fit firmly. To prevent it from becoming dirty, the bandaged tail can then be folded up and secured with a rubber band.

Travel essentials

Your pony's tack, plus saddle soap, sponges, etc., to give it a final clean up

Your riding clothes if you are going to a show

Food and water —for both you and your pony!

Any documents you may need—tickets, entry forms, etc.

First-aid kit for both of you

Loading your pony

Most ponies will walk up the ramp of a van or trailer happily, but if yours is unhappy about it, let it take its time. If it still hesitates, ask a helper to put one of the pony's front feet on the ramp. It will then usually walk in without a problem. Food may help.

Walk confidently up the ramp.

Don't pull your pony.

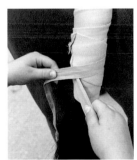
Reward your pony when it goes in.

Ready to go

A single pony in a double trailer travels better on the side closer to the center of the road—this trailer *(above)* is in the U.K. In the U.S. a pony on its own should ride on the left. The other side can hold luggage.

Unloading your pony

Untie the pony leaving its rope through the ring so it thinks it is still tied up. If your trailer has a front ramp *(above)*, put it down, remove the tail strap, and lead the pony down the ramp slowly. To unload from the back, ask a helper to stand at the side to keep the pony moving straight back.

4 Wrap the bandage over the folded-down end to prevent it from slipping.

5 Continue bandaging down the tail until you reach the end of the dock.

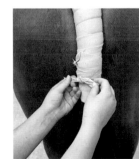

6 Cross the strings, take them around to the back, and cross them again.

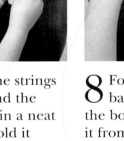

7 Tie the strings around the bandage in a neat bow to hold it securely in place.

8 Fold a layer of bandage over the bow to stop it from coming undone.

Removing a tail bandage

To remove the tail bandage, unfold the part over the bow, untie the strings, and slide the whole thing off in one movement, laying the hair flat and smooth as you do. Roll up the bandage from the strings' end with the strings folded inside.

Summer and winter care

Extremes of temperature and weather may mean that a horse or pony requires special care. In the hot summer weather horses seek shade and an escape from the flies that can make their lives miserable. In the depths of winter a pasture-kept pony will have little to eat, and the ground may be muddy or frozen. The water supply may freeze up, too. We have to solve all of these problems.

Preventing sunburn

Horses and ponies that have pink noses can suffer from sunburn. It particularly affects stabled animals, who may stand with their heads over the stable door for hours in the sun. You can protect them from sunburn by applying sunblock made for use on human skin.

Fly fringe
A fly fringe can be fitted over a halter or worn on its own. As the horse moves, the strings keep flies out of its eyes.

Fly repellent
A number of products are available to help keep flies off. Some are poured onto a cloth and wiped on the pony's coat. Some ponies do not mind spray products.

Coping with flies

Horses and ponies that suffer greatly from flies are best stabled in the daytime and turned out at night. If this is not possible, then fly fringes or fly masks, which cover most of the face, can help. Horses provide their own protection by standing in pairs nose to tail, each swishing the flies off the other's face.

Leg and foot care

In the winter a horse's or pony's legs and feet need special attention. Constant exposure to wet and mud can cause cracks and soreness, called mud fever (page 123), that may become infected, so it is worth trying to protect them from this. Riding on ice is dangerous, but you can ride in snow if you grease its feet.

Leg greasing
Applying petroleum jelly to a horse's lower legs and heels helps protect them from the mud and wet.

Foot greasing
Putting grease in the hoof stops snow from getting inside it.

Keeping warm
A clipped horse or pony will stay warm in the coldest weather if it has sufficient food and if it wears a thick blanket. It is better to add an undersheet or another blanket for warmth than to shut the top half of a Dutch door.

Breaking the ice
In severe weather the water in pasture troughs and even in stalls will freeze. To ensure that your pony has enough to drink, you must break the ice several times a day. If possible, use warm water to fill up the troughs, because this will refreeze less quickly.

Essential winter care

Native ponies can live outdoors without blankets all winter if they have enough to eat. Depending on the weather, the pasture, the pony, and its work, it will need hay and possibly concentrated feed from midwinter to spring.

Health care

H orses—and especially ponies—are hardy animals. Provided you follow a few simple rules, they stay healthy. However, things can go wrong, so you need to know how to cope when they do.

Pricked ears
Although ears laid back are a sign of bad temper rather than sickness, pricked ears show that the pony is interested in what is happening. Its ears move to catch the slightest sound.

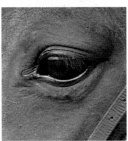

Bright eyes
A pony's eyes should be bright and clear. The pupils should dilate in the dark and contract in bright light. The eyes should not run, though a small amount of dirt may collect in the corners.

Dry nose
A horse's nose should be dry. Some animals that are allergic to dust may have a slight, watery nasal discharge. But thick mucus, especially if greenish or yellow, is a sign of infection.

Other things to check

A healthy horse or pony should be neither fat nor thin. Ribs sticking out and a pot belly are signs of worms, and so is a cough. The horse's breathing should be relaxed and regular—noisy breathing may be a sign of lung disease or dust allergies. When resting, the horse should feel warm with cool feet and legs. Its droppings should be firm balls and just break on reaching the ground.

Signs of good health

A healthy pony has bright eyes, a shiny coat, a hearty appetite, and is interested in everything that goes on around it. Ponies are inquisitive and will come and investigate what you are doing. In a pasture they stay together in a group. A pony that stays away from the others may not be well.

Signs of poor health

If a pony stands with its head down, looking unhappy; if its eyes are dull and its coat is in poor condition, it may be sick. Pinch its skin between your finger and thumb. It should spring straight back into place. If it does not, the pony may be dehydrated (lacking water).

Full of life

Although horses and ponies in a pasture spend most of the time grazing, they will play and gallop around, especially if they are young. This helps them exercise and also keeps them healthy. They only sleep for about four hours a day, and one always stands guard while the others lie down. Horses and ponies can also doze standing up.

Health routines

Regular worming and vaccinations are essential to help keep a horse or pony healthy. It is important to know your pony's usual pulse, temperature, and respiration (breathing) rates, and also to be able to recognize its normal behavior. Being aware of these things will help you find anything that is wrong and fix it quickly.

The vet watches the pony move. If it drags a hind toe, this may indicate lameness in that leg.

Checking the pulse and respiration

Feel for the pulse with your fingers just under the pony's jawbone. Count the number of beats you feel in one minute. It should be 35 to 45 when the pony is resting. The pony's respiration rate is 10 to 20 breaths a minute when resting.

Checking legs

A pony's legs should feel cool and be free from swelling. By running your hand down each leg one at a time every day, you will be able to feel any swelling or heat, which may indicate an injury even if the pony does not seem lame.

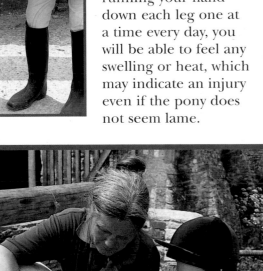

Trotting in hand is the easiest way to check for lameness.

Lameness

If you walk or trot a horse or pony on hard ground, such as concrete, it is possible for someone watching to tell on which leg it is lame. With foreleg lameness, a pony will nod its head as the sound front leg hits the ground.

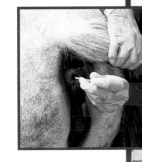

Keep a firm hold of the thermometer for two minutes before you withdraw and read it. Make sure you do not let go!

Taking the temperature

If you think your pony may be sick, ask an adult to help you take its temperature. The normal temperature for a horse or pony is between 99–100°F. Grease the bulb of the thermometer and insert it gently into the pony's rectum.

Worming

Horses and ponies need to be wormed every four to eight weeks. The wormer may be a powder, which you sprinkle in your pony's food, or a paste, which is squirted onto its tongue with an applicator. Ponies don't seem to mind the taste. You should ask an adult to help you worm your pony.

Care of the teeth

Horses' and ponies' back teeth often wear unevenly, making the mouth uncomfortable. It is a good idea to have them checked each year by a vet or an equine dentist. He or she will rasp smooth any sharp edges, using a gag to keep the pony's mouth open and to avoid being bitten.

Gauze

Wound powder | Iodine | Antiseptic solution

Petroleum jelly

Sheet cotton

Poultice | Bandages | Sterile gauze sponges

Worming paste

Round-ended scissors | Thermometers

First-aid kit

It is a good idea to have a first-aid kit handy. Keep it in a clean, dry place, and check it from time to time. If you use any of the contents, replace them so they will be there the next time you need to use them in an emergency.

First aid

It is useful to know how to carry out basic first-aid routines to help you deal with a horse's or pony's minor injuries and problems yourself. But if a pony shows obvious signs of sickness, or is lame or badly injured, you should seek the advice of a knowledgeable adult, because it may be necessary to contact the vet. Prompt veterinary attention can prevent a problem from getting worse.

Preventing infection

Thorough cleaning of a wound will prevent infection and help it heal quickly. Clip off the surrounding hair. Pour warm water into a clean container and add some antiseptic. Dip sterile gauze sponges into the solution, squeeze them out, and use them to clean the wound. Use more gauze sponges until the wound is clean. If the wound bleeds a lot, or is near a joint or tendon, call the vet.

Be sure to use sterile gauze sponges.

Clean the wound from the center out.

Hosing the legs

Hosing down an injured leg with cold water can reduce swelling and pain. Ask a helper to hold the pony and just trickle the hose on its leg to start. Then hose down the leg for about 15 minutes, stop, let it warm up again, and then repeat the process once or twice more.

Applying wound powder

You can treat minor cuts and scratches with antiseptic wound powder, which you sprinkle onto the wound after cleaning it. As well as helping to prevent infections, wound powder helps keep flies away.

Leg bandages

Bandages may be used to hold a dressing in place, support injured or swollen legs, and keep cold, wet legs warm. Bandages are put over a layer of sheet cotton. When bandaging the legs, crouch—do not kneel—beside it.

1 Bandage any dressing, then wrap sheet cotton around the leg. Cover the coronet and make sure the cotton is kept flat.

2 Start applying the bandage just below the knee or hock. Hold the end in place until you have secured it with a few more turns.

1 Cut the poultice to the size you need, and soak it in either hot or cold water. Squeeze out the water while keeping the poultice flat.

2 Place the poultice over the sole of the pony's hoof and start to bandage it in place. It is easiest to use a stretchy, self-adhesive bandage.

3 Bandage in a figure-eight shape around the hoof. When you have finished, tape a thick cotton bandage or a bag around the hoof.

Soaking a foot

Soaking involves putting a horse's foot and lower leg in a low-sided, rubber bucket of warm water with Epsom salts. This is used to help draw out hoof infections. The horse needs to stand with its leg in the bucket for 10–15 minutes, preferably twice a day. Unless the horse is quiet, ask an adult to help.

Applying a poultice

Poultices may be used hot or cold. A hot poultice is used to draw out infection from a wound or abscess; a cold one to reduce swelling, for example, when the foot is bruised. You can buy chemically-prepared poultices made of cotton and gauze.

Finished poultice bandage

3 Work down the leg and over the fetlock and pastern until you reach the top of the hoof. Try to keep the tension even as you work.

4 When you reach the coronet, apply the bandage in the opposite direction and work your way back up the pony's leg.

5 By the time you reach the end of the bandage, you should have arrived back at the place on the leg where you began.

6 Secure the bandage with Velcro straps or tapes. Tie the tapes neatly on the inside or the outside of the pony's leg.

7 The finished bandage should be firm, but not too tight. You should be able to see a layer of sheet cotton at its top and bottom.

Common ailments

Even the best-cared-for horse or pony will occasionally suffer from a minor ailment. Once you can recognize what is wrong you can carry out simple treatments. Look for signs of abnormal behavior in your pony, for areas of sore, rubbed skin, for lumps and swellings, and for any signs of lameness. Laminitis and colic are the most serious problems you are likely to encounter. Both can be caused by a pony overeating.

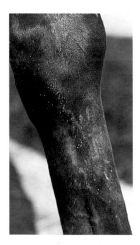

Botfly eggs

Little yellow specks on a pony's lower legs in the summer are botfly eggs. Ask an adult to scrape them off with a botfly knife. If the pony licks the eggs, bot larvae develop in its mouth and stomach. Worming with ivermectin in the early winter destroys the botfly larvae.

Rubbing mane

Even if they do not have sweet itch, many horses and ponies rub their manes and tails in the summer, which looks unpleasant and causes soreness. Rub in medicated shampoo or lotion or protect the horse with a special lightweight, hooded blanket and a fly mask for the face.

Sweet itch

Sweet itch is the name of an allergy from the bites of biting midges, which causes some ponies to rub themselves raw to try and get rid of the irritation. The mane and tail are usually affected.

The midges mostly bite early in the morning and at dusk, so the best way to avoid sweet itch with a susceptible pony is to keep it in its stall at these times.

Medicated shampoo or lotion from a vet or tack shop rubbed into the roots of the mane and tail helps relieve sweet itch.

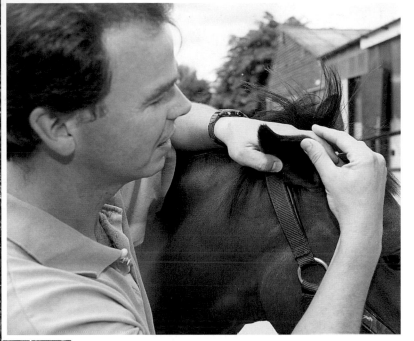

Ear plaques
Areas of white skin in the ears, called plaques, are harmless and do not need treatment.

Looking for mites
You may not see the mites, which are tiny, but thick, brown wax in the ears gives them away.

Problems with a pony's ears

Shaking of the head, rubbing of the ears, and a discharge from the ears are all signs of ear problems. The symptoms may simply be the result of ear mites (tiny parasites), but they could also indicate an infection. If you suspect something is wrong with a pony's ears, have them examined by a vet.

Symptoms of colic

Colic is a common digestive problem, and can be very serious. Affected ponies often roll, but then do not shake themselves afterward. They may lie down and get up again frequently. If badly affected, they will sweat and be in obvious pain. If you see signs of colic, call the vet immediately.

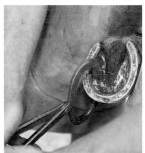

Mud fever
Sore, cracked heels need treatment by a vet.

Hoof testers
Check for laminitis by applying pressure.

Mud fever and laminitis

Mud fever is a winter hoof ailment; ponies that eat too much rich, summer grass can get laminitis, a very painful inflammation of the hoof. It usually affects the front feet, which feel hot, and the pony may be lame. If a pony has symptoms of laminitis, get it in from the pasture and call the vet.

Swollen leg
This swelling on the lower leg might be the result of a knock or a sprain. Hosing down the leg (page 120) may help.

Swellings in the legs

Swellings can be caused by ligament or tendon injuries, bruising, splints (bony enlargements), arthritis, and other conditions. They may feel hard or soft, there may be heat in the leg, and the pony may be lame. It is generally best to seek veterinary advice.

Caring for a sick pony

Asick or injured pony that is confined to its stall likes to follow its normal routine as much as possible. Provided the pony is not too ill, you can give it a light daily grooming. Keep it warm with blankets if necessary, and make sure it always has clean water to drink. If it cannot go out at all, pick the pony a few handfuls of grass to eat each day, as long as the vet allows it. Never feed a pony lawn cuttings.

Giving a pony medicine

Medicines come in different forms—powders, pills, and liquids. Powders and liquids can be mixed in the feed. Putting them in a tasty, moist food, such as applesauce, and mixing it into their feed helps disguise the taste. Pills can be crushed between two spoons and fed in the same way. Liquids may be dropped onto the horse's tongue or inside the lower lip, or squirted into the mouth with a syringe.

Hide a pill or capsule in an apple slice. Cut a slit in the apple and push the pill down into it so the pulp of the fruit surrounds the pill and masks the taste.

Powdered medicine can be sprinkled onto a slice of bread with molasses. Fold the bread to hide the powder and tear or cut it into bite-sized pieces.

Convalescence

A horse or pony confined to a stall for a long time gets very bored, especially when it is feeling better. Divide its hay ration into several smaller nets to keep it occupied. Visit the pony frequently, and bring treats with you. Some horses and ponies like a radio left on for company.

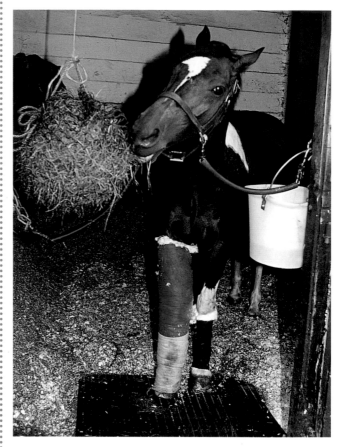

Things to play with

If the horse or pony is allowed to move around, it may enjoy playing with a horse ball. You can buy several types of horse toys, which are designed to be safe and impossible for the horse to puncture if it bites or kicks them.

Stable toys include hanging balls, on which you can smear molasses.

Feline friend

When a horse or pony has to be confined to its stall for long periods and it has no other equine friends around, it may appreciate the company of a friendly household cat or dog, especially if you cannot visit the pony as often as you would like.

Grazing on the lawn

If your pony cannot go out into the pasture, but is allowed out of its stall, spare a few minutes each day to give it some in-hand grazing, provided the vet allows it.

The road to recovery

Once the pony has recovered from its illness you have to get it strong before it can resume normal work. Start by giving it gentle exercise. A good way to do this is with a few minutes' in-hand walking each day, gradually increasing the time and distance. If you are leading the pony on a road, keep it to the side and walk in the direction of traffic. Position yourself between the pony and the traffic—even if it means you have to lead on the right side.

Wear a helmet and gloves when leading a pony on the road.

A pony should wear a bridle when being led on the road

Wear light-colored or reflective clothing

Before you start

Have you ever watched riders at a horse show or simply practicing in a ring and wished you were there riding with them? You could be. Anyone can learn to ride. You just need lessons.

Why take riding lessons?

Participating in events

You may wish to participate in events—in showing, dressage, hunter paces, or gymkhanas. If you ride well enough, you may not need to own a pony to compete. You might be able to borrow one, or even be asked to ride for someone else.

You may be told that if you have a quiet pony to practice on, you can learn to ride on your own. Up to a point this is true. You may learn how to make the pony move forward, turn, and stop. But compare these simple efforts with the style of a top dressage rider or with the boldness of an eventer, galloping cross-country. Whether this is your dream, or whether you just want to ride for fun, taking riding lessons will be your first step on the road to success as a rider.

Trail rides with friends

Going for a trail ride in the country with your friends is one of the most enjoyable riding activities. You can explore new places, and you may spot all kinds of interesting wildlife because animals are not afraid of horses. Your ponies, too, will enjoy being ridden out in the company of others.

Riding vacations

A riding vacation may mean pony trekking in Scotland, riding out west like a cowboy, exploring the mountains of Spain, or having intensive lessons with a professional. You will have a wonderful time on a riding vacation, and you will enjoy it even more if you are a good rider.

Where to take riding lessons

I t is important to choose a good stable when you decide to take lessons. Look for those that are approved by an equestrian organization. Try to visit several stables, and check what facilities they provide. They should be orderly and have a calm atmosphere.

Friendly instructors

The instructors at a good stable will be friendly and helpful, even if they may sometimes be firm with you! You should be able to ask them questions, and if necessary, talk to them about any difficulties you may have. When they are instructing, the instructors should wear boots and riding hats. They should also wear gloves when they are leading a horse or pony.

Happy horses

A row of clean, shiny heads looking out over their stable doors, taking an interest in everything going on, is a good sign. The ponies should look well fed, and their stalls should be clean. Overall the stables should be swept and organized.

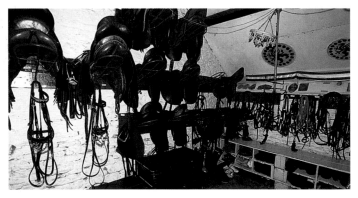

Tidy tack room

Tack has to be clean and well cared for. There should be no cracked leather, fraying girths, or stitching coming undone. Tack should be stored neatly in a tack room, ideally one which is heated in the winter, with the saddles and bridles kept on brackets and hooks.

Lessons in the outdoor arena

The stable will probably have an outdoor arena in which lessons are given. This is a fenced arena that may have a surface of rubber chips or sand, kept raked smooth and level. Even if the arena is just a fenced-off corner of a field, it should not be deep with mud.

Riding surface
The surface of an indoor arena—usually sand—stays dry whatever the weather. It must be raked smooth.

The indoor arena

An indoor arena, usually housed in a large barn, is a great asset to a stable. Whatever the weather, you can stay dry for your lessons. And during the winter it means you can ride in the late afternoons and evenings when it is too dark to ride outside.

Watching lessons
Many indoor arenas have an area where people can sit or stand to watch lessons in progress. If the indoor ring is large enough, the stable may hold competitions in it during the winter.

When work is over

In the summer, at the end of a long day's lessons, the ponies may be turned out into the pasture to enjoy some well-earned freedom. In the winter they are likely to be stabled at night and given feed and hay.

Clothes to wear for riding

Every sport has its competition uniform—in riding this means a shirt, a jacket, jodhpurs, boots, hat, and gloves. When not competing, riders dress more casually. The one essential item on all occasions is a helmet.

Why wear riding gear?

Jodhpurs and boots are more comfortable to wear when riding than jeans and shoes. Jodhpurs stop your legs from rubbing against the saddle; boots protect you from being knocked by the stirrups.

Body protector

For any riding activity that involves jumping you should wear a body protector. It is a rigid vest that protects your back in case you fall off.

Riding gloves with palm grips

Gloves

Riding gloves have special surfaces on their palms to help grip the reins. They may have leather or suede palms or raised rubber spots, which are useful in wet weather when reins become very slippery. You should always wear gloves when you are riding, leading, or lungeing horses and ponies.

Headgear

You must always wear a helmet when riding. You should also wear it when you are leading or lungeing a horse or pony. Whether you choose a schooling helmet or velvet-covered cap, you must make sure it is the right size. It should have a safety harness and comply with the latest safety standards.

A hunt cap has a rigid brim and is covered with fine velvet.

Casual clothes

For riding lessons or going on a trail ride you will be comfortable in jodhpurs, boots, gloves, helmet, and a shirt worn with a sweater or a jacket if the weather is cool.

Adjustable shoulder strap

A schooling helmet is a round, brimless helmet.

Safety harness

Covers are available in various colors to wear over schooling helmets.

Adjust the safety harness so that it is comfortable but holds the hat in place.

Shirt and tie (boys only in the U.S.)

Jacket

Schooling helmet with colorful cover

Fleece under jacket

Western gear

When showing, western riders wear a western-style shirt with a collar, jeans or western-style pants, chaps, and western-style boots with a heel. Many riders dress more casually. To protect their heads, most young riders wear helmets.

Show gear
To compete in a show or any other event you should wear formal riding clothes. You may wear a black or navy blue show jacket.

Winter wear
A quilted, waterproof jacket is ideal for cold days, and half chaps help keep your legs warm. In wet weather a full-length raincoat will keep you dry.

Boots

There are many kinds of boots for riding, including ankle-length, leather jodhpur boots with elasticated sides and tall riding boots, which may be made of leather or a synthetic material, and tie-up paddock boots. Long boots and half chaps protect the inner sides of your legs from being pinched by the stirrup leathers. You can wear other shoes when you are riding, as long as they are strong and have a smooth, non-ridged sole and a heel.

Jodhpur boots protect your ankles.

Riding boots reach almost up to your knees and fit tightly.

Leather half chaps may fasten with straps or zips.

Measuring a pony

Traditionally, horses and ponies are measured in hands. One hand is equal to about 4 in. (10cm), which is roughly the width of an adult's hand.

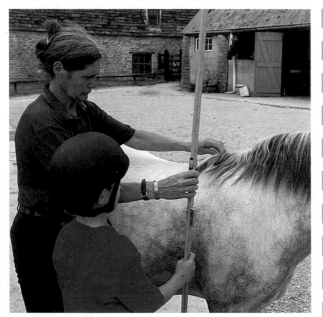

A measuring stick
An upright pole with a sliding bar enables you to read off the pony's height.

On the withers
The horizontal sliding bar rests on the highest point of the pony's withers.

Types of ponies

Ponies may be a variety of shapes and sizes. They can be so stocky and broad that your legs barely reach around them, or they may be tall and narrow. They can be hard to keep moving, or they can go like the wind. For your first lessons you need a quiet pony. As your riding improves you may step up to a more lively one.

The right-sized pony

It is important that the pony you ride is the right size for you. If the pony is too large or too small, you will be unable to use your legs properly to give the correct aids, and you may find it more difficult to balance. If you are too large for the pony, you may also be too heavy for it to carry you, and you could injure its back.

Too small a pony
This pony is too small for its rider. The rider's legs are too long to make proper contact with the pony's sides, and she may also be too heavy for the pony.

Too large a horse
This horse is much too large for its rider. The girl's legs do not reach far enough down its sides for her to be able to give the aids in the right place behind the girth.

The right size
This pony and its rider are just the right size for each other. The soles of the rider's feet are level with the line of the pony's belly, so she can give the aids properly.

A variety of ponies

During your riding career you will meet many ponies. Physically they will range from the hairy-heeled native type to the elegant, lightly-built thoroughbred type. Most will not be pure bred. Their temperaments will vary too, from sluggish to highly excitable. Some ponies will need more experienced riders than others.

Crossbred pony
A crossbred pony means that its parents are from different breeds. For example its mother is a welsh pony, and its father is a quarter horse. This pony would suit a competent rider and could carry out most activities.

Thoroughbred-type show pony
This kind of pony has beautiful gaits and goes well in the show ring. It would need an experienced rider.

Typical beginner's pony
A first pony might be a native breed or crossbred. It will be quiet and dependable.

Purebred native pony
A pony such as this Welsh Section A (Welsh Mountain) is an ideal all-rounder for a fairly experienced rider.

A pony's tack

Tack means the saddle, bridle, and the other equipment used on a horse or pony. Tack is usually made from leather, with stainless steel bits and stirrups.

Saddles and girths

You need a saddle to give you a secure and comfortable seat on a horse's back. The girth holds the saddle in place. Saddles are made on a rigid frame called a tree. A canvas seat is stretched across the tree and the padded seat goes over that. Saddles are made in different sizes and widths to fit horses of different sizes.

Types of saddles

Saddles are made in different styles according to the use for which they are intended. Mostly you will use some kind of general purpose saddle, but if you go on to take part in equestrian sports, you may need to use a special saddle.

Cantle
Seat
Pommel
Gullet
D ring
Lining
Waist
Skirt
Surcingle loop (keeper)
Saddle flap
Saddle flap
Billets
Buckle guard

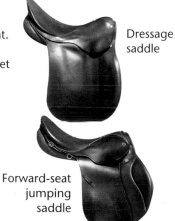

A dressage saddle has straight flaps and a deep seat. It often has extended billets so that the buckles do not get in the way of the rider's leg contact with the horse.

Dressage saddle

A forward-seat jumping saddle has forward-cut flaps and padding in front of the rider's knees (knee rolls) and behind their thighs (thigh rolls) to help keep their legs in the right position when jumping.

Forward-seat jumping saddle

A general purpose saddle has moderately forward-cut flaps and slight padding in front of the rider's knees. It is comfortable and suitable for most riding activities.

Types of girths

Girths may be made from leather, webbing, or synthetic fibers. Webbing girths were traditionally used in pairs. Leather girths, which may be made from a folded piece of leather or shaped to avoid pinching near the horse's elbows, are expensive but last a long time. String girths are inexpensive but can pinch the horse's skin. Padded synthetic girths are comfortable and easy to maintain. For safety, girths should be fastened on either the front two or the front and back billets.

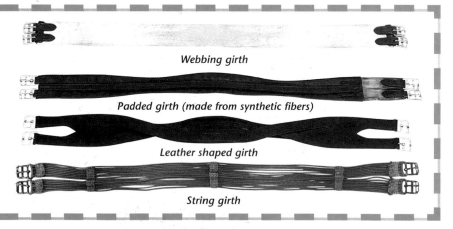

Webbing girth

Padded girth (made from synthetic fibers)

Leather shaped girth

String girth

Halters

Halters are put on horses' or ponies' heads to lead them and to tie them up. They may be made of nylon or leather. People tend to use nylon halters around the stable and keep leather ones for special occasions.

The lead rope clips to the ring under the pony's chin.

Bridles and bits

A bridle and bit are the means by which a horse or pony is controlled by its rider. Bridles are traditionally made of leather in three sizes: full size, cob, and pony. Today other materials are also used. There are two main kinds of bits—snaffle and curb—though there are many different varieties. Bits are usually made of stainless steel.

Snaffle bridle

A snaffle bridle, which has a jointed snaffle bit and single reins, is the kind most often used. The headpiece buckles onto cheekpieces, which hold the bit in place. A separate headpiece is attached to the noseband and fastens on the left.

Throatlatch stops the bridle from slipping forward.

Cheekpiece holds the bit in place.

Noseband

Stop, to keep the ring of a running martingale away from the bit.

Eggbutt snaffle bit

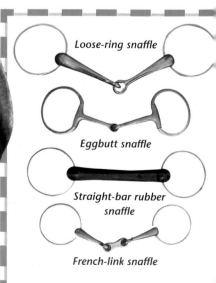

Loose-ring snaffle

Eggbutt snaffle

Straight-bar rubber snaffle

French-link snaffle

Browband   Headpiece

Double bridle

A double bridle has both a snaffle bit and a curb bit and two pairs of reins. It is used only on well-trained horses and ponies by experienced riders. The snaffle bit, or bridoon, raises the horse's head. The curb bit lowers the horse's head. The curb chain, tightening in the chin groove, gives extra control.

Bridoon cheekpiece

Curb chain

Weymouth (curb) bit

Curb rein

Bridoon (snaffle) rein

Bit converters

Short leather straps that connect the curb and bridoon rings of a pelham bit, allowing single reins to be used with it, are called bit converters. Their use means that the two functions of the bit cannot be separated, but some horses go well with them.

Running martingale

This attaches to the girth at one end. It passes through a neck strap and then divides into two straps that end in rings through which the reins pass.

Types of bits

A snaffle bit consists of a mouthpiece—usually jointed—and two rings. A curb bit has cheekpieces that rotate to put pressure on the headpiece of the bridle. It also has a curb chain, which presses on the curb groove and is held down by a lip-strap.

A kimberwick bit, which acts like a single-rein pelham, is useful for a strong pony.

The two bits of a double bridle are the bridoon (snaffle) and Weymouth (curb).

A half-moon pelham combines the actions of the snaffle and curb bits. It would be used with a curb chain.

Standing martingale

Like a running martingale, this also attaches to the girth and passes through a neck strap, but the single strap is then fastened to the back of the noseband of the pony's bridle.

Martingales

Martingales are used to stop a horse carrying his head too high and evading the rider's control. They also prevent it from throwing its head up in the air and possibly hitting the rider in the face. They should be fitted with care. They must not be so tight that they pull the horse's head down.

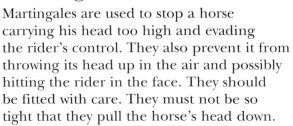

Saddle blanket

The horse wears a thick woolen blanket or pad under the saddle to protect its back from being rubbed. Traditionally these blankets were handwoven from sheep's wool and doubled as bedrolls.

Western saddle

A traditional western saddle weighs 40–50 lbs (18–22.5kg). Most modern saddles are lighter, but they all feature the horn at the front, to which steers were roped, and the high cantle at the back. The girth is called a cinch.

Western tack

Western tack was designed for a cowboy's horse. The saddle was the cowboy's home. It had to be comfortable and carry belongings—from bedding and food supplies to ropes and a rifle. The bridle had long reins. When they trailed on the ground, the horse was trained to stand still as if tied up.

Horn — Cantle

— Flank strap

— Skirt

— Fender made of decorative leather

Seat jockey

Front rigging

Under the saddle flap
When you lift the saddle flap, you can see the broad, leather strap that carries the stirrup. The outer fender covers the strap and protects the rider's leg.

Western stirrups
A stirrup is made from a single, curved piece of wood or plastic.

Putting on the saddle

If you are small, you may need help to carry and put on a western saddle. It takes a lot of strength to lift it up onto a horse's back and settle it in place. Never "throw" the saddle on, like you see in some movies, because this would upset the horse.

1 First put the saddle blanket on, and then lower the saddle onto the horse's back.

2 Check that the cinch is not twisted on the right side, and then fasten it on the left side.

3 The cinch may be buckled or tied in place. Once you have fastened it tuck in the free end of the leather.

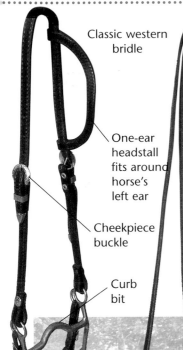

Classic western bridle

One-ear headstall fits around horse's left ear

Cheekpiece buckle

Curb bit

Types of western bridles

Instead of a browband, most western bridles have a loop that fits around one of the ears to stop the headpiece from slipping. For a trained horse, the bridle usually has a curb bit with a port (the half-moon shape in the center). A hackamore controls the horse without a bit.

Putting on the bridle
With the bridle in your right hand and your right arm under the horse's jaw, press the bit into its mouth with your left hand.

Western hackamore
A hackamore is a type of bitless bridle. It uses a heavy, braided rawhide noseband, called a bosal, to control the horse.

Western bridles rarely have a noseband when the bridle has a bit.

Reins

Seat of saddle

Horn

Headstall

Long-cheeked curb bit

Saddle strings tie the rider's belongings onto the saddle.

Cinch is made from woven hair or cord

All tacked up

The horse is now ready to be ridden. It is wearing a lightweight, modern western saddle over a colorful saddle blanket. The long reins, which do not fasten together, are looped over the horse's neck to stop them from dragging on the ground.

A pony's halter

Halters are made either of leather or nylon. They are used to lead a horse or pony and to tie it up. Like bridles, they are made in three basic sizes—pony, cob, and full-size. A very small pony may need a foal halter, which has a number of adjustable straps.

A good fit

This leather halter fits well. It fastens on the pony's left side, and the lead rope is clipped to the round ring under its chin.

Too small

This halter was made to fit a much smaller pony. The headpiece does not even reach far enough to meet the buckle on the cheekpiece.

Too large

This halter is much too large. The pony could pull its head back through it and escape, or get a foot caught in it when grazing or scratching.

Checking the size

A halter needs to fit correctly in the same way as a bridle does. There should be room for you to insert two fingers under the noseband and a hand under the throatlash. A halter that is too tight, especially if it is made of nylon, will rub and may cause sores over the pony's prominent nasal bones.

Fitting and caring for tack

T ack is a horse's or pony's saddle, bridle, halter, and any other saddlery it may wear, such as a martingale. In order for the tack to work correctly, it must fit well, be correctly adjusted, and be well cared for. Neglected tack is dangerous. It can give the pony sores and may break, leading to accidents.

There should be two fingers' width under the noseband.

Bit

Throatlatch

Well-fitting bridle

This pony is wearing a well-fitting snaffle bridle with an eggbutt snaffle bit. The browband is at the correct height so it does not pinch the pony's ears, the noseband and throatlash fit well, and the bit just wrinkles the corners of the pony's mouth.

Storing tack

Tack should be cleaned before it is put away. Bridles are hung on arched racks that do not bend the headpieces; saddles are supported on brackets attached to the wall or on free-standing saddle horses.

You should see daylight between the saddle and the spine.

Saddle panel

Fitting a saddle

Horses and ponies vary a lot in shape and size, and it is important that the saddle fits well. It must be the right width, and the panel stuffing must be even so the leather maintains a level contact with the pony's back. The saddle must not press on the pony's spine or the withers.

Tacking up

Check that the saddle pad does not press down on the pony's withers. You should be able to insert three fingers between the withers and the pommel of the saddle and two between the girth and the pony.

How to clean tack

It is important to keep saddle and bridle leather clean and supple. If you do so, it will last for many years. You should clean it each time you use it. To clean tack, you need a bucket of warm water, one sponge for cleaning off the dirt and oil, one sponge for saddle-soaping, and a bar of saddle soap.

Wash the bit in clean water and dry it. Clean all the oil and mud off of the bridle with a slightly damp sponge. Then dip the bar of saddle soap into the water and rub it onto your other sponge.

Rub saddle soap well into the leather, undoing fasteners so no parts of the bridle are neglected. Keep moistening the soap when you need more on the sponge. When you have finished, refasten all the buckles.

Wipe any mud off the stirrup irons with your cleaning sponge. Rinse the sponge, squeeze it as dry as possible, and clean the oil off of the underside of the saddle, as well as any mud. Do not get the leather too wet.

If you wet the sponge when you are using saddle soap, you will have too much lather. Moisten the soap instead. Rub the sponge all over the saddle. Don't forget the girth billets and stirrup leathers.

Tying a quick-release knot

When tying up a pony, fasten its lead rope to a loop of string or a ring using a quick-release knot.

Loop the lead rope, and put it through the ring. Twist the rope a few times.

Make another loop in the end of the rope, and push it through the first loop.

Tighten the knot by pulling on the halter end. Pull the free end to undo it.

Putting on a halter

You will need to put a halter on a pony in the stall so you can tie it up while you are grooming, tacking up, and mucking out. You will also need to use a halter to catch the pony and lead it back from the pasture.

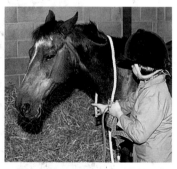

1 If the pony is outside or if it is likely to wander around the stall, first put the lead rope around its neck so you can hold on to it if you need to do so.

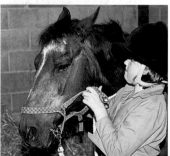

2 Put the noseband over its nose. Hold the cheekpiece of the halter in your left hand. Reach under its chin with your right hand to grasp the headpiece.

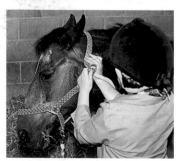

3 Bring the headpiece over the pony's head and fasten the buckle, tucking in the end of the strap. Tie up the pony using a quick release knot.

Saddling up

When you have your first riding lessons, your pony will be tacked up for you—that means it will have its saddle and bridle on. But you will need to learn how to do this by yourself. Start by tying the pony up in the stable or its stall, and then get its tack. You can hang the bridle on a hook or over the door while you saddle up.

Carry the bridle over your shoulder.

Carry the saddle over your arm with the pommel resting by your elbow.

Run the stirrups up the leathers.

Carry the girth over the saddle.

Carrying tack

To avoid trailing the reins on the ground, loop them up and put them with the bridle over your shoulder. Carry the saddle on your left arm, supporting it with your right hand. It is then in position for saddling the pony.

Putting on a saddle

The saddle sits just behind the pony's withers, and the girth goes around in the shallow groove just behind its forelegs. You put the saddle on from the pony's left side, but you must go around to the right side to fasten on the saddle pad and check that the girth is correctly buckled on that side and not twisted.

1 Hold the saddle pad in both hands, and lower it onto the pony's back in front of where it will eventually go.

2 Put the saddle on top of the saddle pad, and then slide them back together until they are in the right position.

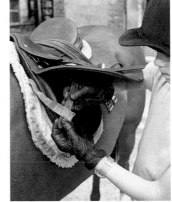

3 Take the front billet out of the buckle guard and slide it through the loop on the saddle pad's strap.

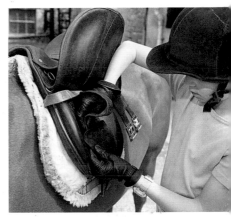

4 Put the front billet back through the buckle guard. Repeat steps three and four on the left side of the saddle.

5 Let the girth hang down on the right side, and check that it is not twisted.

6 Go back to the left side of the pony, and reach underneath its belly to grab hold of the end of the girth.

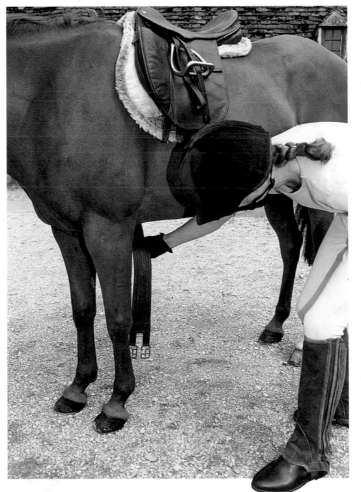

7 Fasten the girth buckles on the front two or the front and back billets. Smooth the skin under the girth.

Slide the guard back down over the girth buckles.

Putting on a bridle

A horse's or pony's head is very sensitive, so you must always handle it gently when putting on its bridle. Be careful not to brush your arm or the bridle's cheekpieces against its eyes. Do not pull on its mouth when you put in the bit. If you do it slowly and gently, putting on a bridle is not as difficult as it may appear.

How to put on a bridle

When you are learning, a bridle appears to be a very complicated piece of equipment. The key to being able to put it on without getting confused is to hold it up by the headpiece and take a good look at it. The headpiece goes over the top of the pony's head, and the cheekpieces support the bit. The browband stops the headpiece from slipping back, and the throatlatch stops the bridle from slipping forward.

1 Carrying the bridle, approach the pony on its left side and undo its halter. Slip the halter off its head, and then refasten the headpiece around the pony's neck.

Checking the fit

A horse or pony usually wears the same bridle each time it is ridden, so it should fit properly without needing much adjustment. But you need to know how the bridle should fit to be sure it is correct.

Before you put the bridle on check that the noseband is level. If it is not, straighten it out by easing the headpiece through the browband, pushing it up on one side, and pulling it down on the other.

The cheekpieces should be buckled onto the bridle's headpiece at the same number hole on each side. If they are not, the bit will be pulled up more on one side than on the other.

When the noseband fits correctly, it should lie halfway between the pony's cheekbone and its mouth. There should be enough room for you to slide two fingers between the noseband and the pony's nose.

When you have fastened the throatlatch, there should be room for your whole hand to pass between it and the pony's cheek. If the throatlash is too tight, it may interfere with the pony's breathing.

A snaffle bit should slightly wrinkle the corners of a pony's mouth when it is at the correct height. You can adjust the height of the bit by altering the length of the cheekpieces on each side of the bridle.

6 Pull out the pony's forelock from under the browband so it lies nicely over it. Smooth out any parts of the mane that are caught in the headpiece.

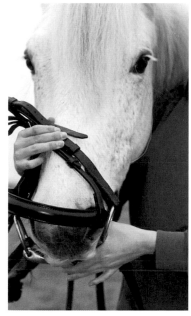

2 Hold the bridle in your left hand by the headpiece. Take hold of the reins in your right hand, and put them over the pony's neck.

3 Put your right arm under the pony's jaw, and hold the bridle in your right hand. Holding the bit flat on your outstretched left hand, press it against the pony's lips.

4 If the pony does not want to open its mouth, wiggle your left thumb in the corner where it has no teeth. Press the bit against its lips as you do so.

5 When the bit is in the pony's mouth, put the bridle's headpiece over its ears, folding the ears down to enable you to do so.

7 On both sides of the bridle, check that the browband is not so high up that it is pressing against the base of the pony's ears.

8 Reach under the pony's jaw to the right-hand side of the bridle for the throatlash. Check it is not twisted, and then bring it under to the left side of the bridle, and fasten the buckle.

9 Check that the bridle's noseband is not caught up on the cheekpieces, and then fasten it behind the pony's jaw. Push the end of the noseband strap firmly through its keeper.

10 Do a final check on the bridle. Make sure that the buckles are fastened correctly and the ends of all the straps are in their keepers.

First lessons

The first time you sit on a pony you will probably feel a little strange. As you have more lessons you will begin to feel at home on its back. Your first pony will be a very quiet one, and it will help your instructor take care of you.

Meeting your pony

W hen you go for your first riding lesson, your instructor will introduce you to the pony you are going to ride. It is a very exciting moment—although you may feel a little nervous. If you do, try to hide it from the pony. Ponies quickly sense how someone is feeling and react to it. If you are anxious and upset, or worried, your pony will become anxious too. If you act in a positive way, your pony will have confidence in you.

Greeting a new friend

When you meet a strange pony, walk up to it confidently. Hold out the back of your hand with your fingers curled into your palm, and let it sniff at it. Speak to the pony, and give it a pat on the neck.

Getting ready

If you are having a group lesson, you will probably lead your pony to the arena and then mount there. Before you mount, you or your instructor should check the pony's tack. Your instructor will probably help you mount by holding the pony.

Setting off

If you mount before the arena, the group will set off for the arena when all the riders are on their ponies and have checked their girths and the length of their stirrups (pages 154–155).

Your first lessons

You may have private riding lessons or lessons with a group of other beginners. Either way, your instructor or an assistant may lead your pony with a lead line. This clips on to the pony's bit rings, leaving you to hold the bridle's reins.

Getting to know a pony

Before you can handle and ride ponies you need to know a little about them. Ponies are gentle, nervous animals, happiest in a group. If something frightens them, their instinct is to run away. Living naturally in a herd, they follow a dominant pony. When we domesticate them we take that animal's place, and once they trust us they will do as we wish.

Approach with confidence

When you approach a pony, talk to it in a friendly way. Give it a pat on the neck or a treat, and handle it quietly and firmly. It will then feel confident. If you are nervous, hesitant, or pushy, it will be upset and may behave badly.

How to lead a pony correctly

You lead a pony on its left side. Hold the lead rope or reins in your right hand up by the pony's head, and take the other end in your left hand. Walk forward in a positive way beside the pony's shoulder without looking back at it.

Tips for handling horses and ponies

Speak to a horse or pony in a calm and friendly way as you approach it.

Approach toward its shoulder, from the front, where it can see you.

Never shout, rush around, or make sudden movements near horses or ponies.

Be gentle but firm when you are handling horses and ponies.

Try to follow the same routine around the stable and with the horse each day.

Natural behavior

Wild ponies live in herds. If you turn a pony out in a pasture, it will immediately gallop off to join the others. If one pony shies from an object, the others will copy it.

Nervous or naughty?

A pony that hesitates about passing an unusual object may be frightened. Give it the benefit of the doubt and let it have a good look at the object. Then drive the pony firmly forward with your seat and legs, keeping the pressure on until the pony has passed the object.

Gaining control

Once the pony walks past the object relax your aids, and reward the pony. Pat it on the neck and tell it what a good pony it is. If it refuses to pass the object, take the pony around in a circle and approach it again, reinforcing your aids with a crop if necessary.

Mounting block

Mounting blocks give you extra height and stop you from pulling the saddle over.

Hold the reins in your left hand, and put your left foot in the stirrup. Spring off your right foot with your right hand holding the saddle.

Swing your right leg over the horse's back, and lower yourself into the saddle. Put your right foot in the stirrup, and then take up the right rein.

Getting a leg up

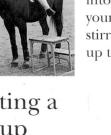

Hold the reins in your left hand, and put your right hand on the saddle. Your helper holds your left leg.

With your helper supporting your left leg below the knee, decide when they will lift (such as on the count of three). Lift yourself with your arms while your helper propels you up.

When you reach the level of the saddle, swing your right leg over it and sit down. Straighten your back, put both your feet in the stirrups, and then take up the reins in both hands.

Mounting

Mounting means getting on a horse or pony. Although you may have help at first, you will need to do it alone. When you are out riding, you may have to dismount to open a gate, for example, and you have to be able to get back on again. If you find mounting difficult because you are not very strong and lack spring or because you are not very tall, try letting the stirrup leather down a hole or two.

How to mount

There are various ways of mounting a pony. You may be able to use a mounting block or to get a leg up, but you will also be taught the correct way to mount. When you are learning, you should have a helper hold your pony. When you are on your own, you can stop your pony from walking forward by standing it to face a wall or gate.

1 Stand on the pony's left side, facing its tail. Hold the reins in your left hand. With your right hand, turn the stirrup toward you and put your left foot in it.

2 With your left hand resting on the pony's withers, grasp the waist of the saddle with your right hand and at the same time spring up off your right foot.

Turning the stirrup

It is important that the stirrup iron and leather are turned the right way when you are riding. If they are not, the edge of the stirrup leather presses into your leg. This is very uncomfortable and prevents you from using your legs properly.

Before you mount, turn the back of the stirrup iron toward you. As you mount and twist your leg and foot around the stirrup turns so it ends up facing the right way.

To put your right foot in the stirrup, turn the front of the iron out. You may do this with your hand at first, but with practice you will be able to use your foot.

Western style

Start by facing the horse's left side. Hold the reins in your left hand, resting on the horn of the saddle. Put your left foot in the stirrup and your right hand on the back of the saddle. Spring up off your right foot. Swing your right leg over, being careful not to catch it on the high cantle. Lower yourself gently into the saddle. Put your right foot in the stirrup, and take the reins in your right hand.

3 Swing your right leg up and over the pony's back, being careful not to kick it with your toe as you do so. It is helpful if someone leans on your right stirrup as you mount to stop you from pulling the saddle over to the left when all your weight is on that side.

4 As you bring your right leg over the saddle, slide your right hand out of the way. Lower yourself down gently—do not flop.

5 Slip your right foot into the right stirrup, pointing your toe in as you do so. Take up the reins in both of your hands.

Dismounting

The method of dismounting that starts with both feet out of the stirrups involves a certain amount of gymnastics. Most people consider it the best way to get off a horse because it is the safest. The most dangerous thing that can happen to a rider is to be dragged along the ground by a moving horse because one foot is stuck in a stirrup. By taking both feet out of the stirrups and then jumping clear, you land on both feet at the same time and can walk with the horse.

How to dismount

When dismounting, you vault off the pony in one easy movement, so you have both feet on the ground very quickly and can walk beside the pony if it moves. As you land beside the pony be careful to keep your own feet out of the way of its front hooves so it does not tread on you. Before you dismount, check that you are not going to land on uneven ground and risk hurting your feet or ankles when they take your weight.

1 Bring the pony up to a good, square halt (page 160) on a level piece of ground. If you think it may walk forward, face a gate. Still holding the reins in both hands, take both feet out of the stirrups.

1 Hold the reins in your left hand, and put your right hand on the pommel. Then take your right foot out of the stirrup.

Alternative way

An alternative method is to take your right foot out of the stirrup first and then vault off to land on both feet together. Unless the pony is trained to stand, you should get someone to hold it while you dismount this way.

2 Pass the reins and crop, if you are using one, to your left hand. Rest them on the base of the pony's neck, just in front of the withers.

2 Swing your right leg over the pony's back, and put your right hand on the waist of the saddle. Take your left foot out of the stirrup and vault off.

3 Slip to the ground, landing on both feet and bending your knees slightly as you do so. Then with your right hand take hold of the reins by the bit so you can lead the pony.

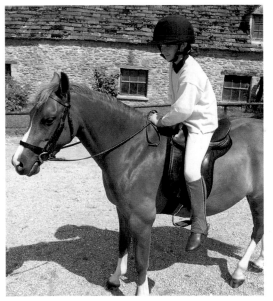

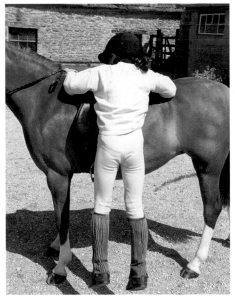

3 While still holding the reins in your left hand, put your right hand on the pommel of the saddle and lean forward.

4 Swing your right leg up and bring it over the pony's back, being careful that you do not kick the pony as you do so.

5 Slip to the ground, landing lightly on both feet and bending your knees. Take hold of the reins near the bit in your right hand.

How to sit in the saddle

W hen you sit on a horse or a pony, you should be relaxed and comfortable yet alert and ready for action. You should sit deep in the saddle with your back straight and your thighs and lower legs in contact with the saddle and the pony. Your body should be supple enough to follow all of its movements.

How to hold the reins

Hold your hands in a relaxed position in front of you with the thumbs up and the palms of your hands facing each other. Then take up the reins. Single reins should pass between your pinky and ring fingers, up through your hands, and between your thumbs and first fingers.

Diagonal line

When you are sitting on the pony your arms must be in the right position. If you are holding the reins correctly, the reins and the lower parts of your arms should form a straight, diagonal line running directly from the pony's bit back to your elbows.

Foot position in stirrup
When you are putting your foot in the stirrup, turn the front edge of the iron out. Rest the ball of your foot on the stirrup iron, and keep your toes pointing forward and your heels pressed down.

Shortening reins

Hold both reins in your right hand while you slide your left hand down to the length you want. Then hold both reins in your left hand, and slide your right hand down to shorten the right rein to the correct length.

Stirrup length

If you sit in the saddle and let your legs hang down naturally, the stirrups will be approximately the correct length when they hit you at your ankles. You may need them a couple of holes shorter than this to start with and when jumping.

Keep your head up and look straight ahead between the pony's ears.

Keep your upper arms relaxed, and hold them close to your body.

Sit up straight, but do not hold your back stiffly.

Keep your seat in contact with the saddle, and do not lean back.

Keep your heels down and your toes up.

Vertical line

When you are sitting in the saddle, imagine a straight vertical line running down beside you. If you are sitting in the correct position, the line would start at your ear and pass down through your shoulder and hip before eventually finishing at the level of your heel.

Checking the girth

You should check the girth before you mount, but it is a good idea to check it again after a few minutes' riding. Some ponies blow themselves out when they are saddled and their girths are being tightened. Later when they have relaxed, the girth may be too loose. You can adjust it from either side.

Keeping hold of the reins, lean forward to slide your fingers under the girth. If you can get more than two fingers between the girth and the pony, then you need to tighten the girth.

Put your left leg forward, lift the saddle flap, and pull up the billets one at a time to tighten them.

Adjusting the stirrup length

You can adjust your stirrups while mounted, keeping your feet in them as you do so. With practice you can do this by touch alone, without looking down.

Holding the reins in one hand, pull up the end of the leather with the other.

Undo the buckle, slide it to the correct position, and put the prong in the hole.

Pull down the underneath part of the leather to slide the buckle up again.

The aids

The aids are the signals a rider uses to communicate their wishes to a horse or pony. The aids are divided into natural aids—the rider's legs, hands, seat, and voice—and artificial aids—crops and spurs. A well-trained horse responds to the lightest of aids, but some ponies may need stronger ones.

Hand position
Keep your fingers closed while you keep an even contact with the horse's mouth.

Boot with spur fitted

Spurs are attached to riding boots with leather straps.

Artificial aids

There are various kinds of crops. Long crops are used for dressage and schooling; short crops for ordinary riding; and leather-covered crops for showing. Both crops and spurs are used to reinforce leg aids, although spurs should be used only by experienced riders.

Dressage crop

Normal crop

Jumping bat

Hand position
Let your fingers relax and keep a loose hold on the reins.

Riding on a loose rein

At the end of a ride and at intervals during a lesson it is a good idea to let the horse walk on a loose rein to stretch its neck muscles and relax. When you are riding on a loose rein, you still need to keep your lower legs in contact with the horse's sides, but you can ease the pressure on the reins. However, you must always be ready to gather up the reins quickly if something startles the horse.

Medium walk

Maintain a feel on the horse's mouth through the reins. With your lower legs, squeeze its sides behind the girth to tell it to walk forward.

Leg position
Keep your heels pointing down and your lower legs pressed into the horse's sides.

Driving forward

Sometimes ponies dislike or are afraid of particular objects and refuse to pass them. When this happens, keep a firm hold of the reins and use your legs really strongly to drive the pony forward.

Using a crop

If the pony does not pay attention to your leg aid, you can reinforce it with a tap of the crop just behind the girth. A pony that misbehaves can also be given a sharp tap with the crop in the same place.

Expert rider

If you watch an expert rider performing a dressage test you will hardly notice any aids being given. The lightest of touches and slight shifts of weight in the saddle are enough to instruct the horse to carry out the most complicated movements.

A dressage rider rides with long stirrups.

This dressage movement is called a piaffe. It is like trotting in place.

"Leg into hand" is the aim of riding. The legs drive the horse forward; the hands control the energy created.

First-time rider

On the lead line the instructor has direct control of the pony. To help the rider feel safe on their first lesson, the instructor will tell them to hold on to the front of the saddle or a neck strap.

On the lunge or lead line

Your first few riding lessons are likely to be on the lunge or on a lead line. The instructor controls your pony, leaving you free to concentrate on sitting correctly and applying the aids. A lunge line is a long rein attached to a special halter that the pony wears over its bridle.

Starting out
As the horse walks around in circles the rider steadies themself by holding on to the front of the saddle.

Gaining confidence
Once the rider feels secure, they let go of the saddle and hold the reins in the correct position.

On the lunge

Riding on the lunge is a good way of learning to balance on the horse and to build up your confidence. It enables you to practice using the aids without having to worry about the horse's speed or direction.

Tips for first lessons

Get comfortable in the saddle before you start. Make sure that your stirrups feel right and that the ends of the leathers are not sticking into your legs.

If you feel insecure, hold on to the front of the saddle or to a neck strap.

Try to relax. Let your hands follow the movement of the pony's head.

Off balance

If you lose your balance when you are first learning to ride, it is tempting to try to hang on by pulling on the reins. You should never do so, however, as you can damage the pony's mouth and may make it very sore.

Trying too hard

When you first ride a horse or pony, you must try to remember many things, but do not try so hard that you hold your body stiffly. Try to sit easily, and let your body and hands follow the horse's movements.

Holding the reins
You can rest your hands on either side of the horse's withers to help you balance.

Halter
The horse may wear a halter to lead it by.

Using your legs
Squeeze with your legs behind the girth to keep the horse walking on.

Walking slowly
At first the instructor will lead the horse around at a slow walk.

On your own

When you first ride off the lunge or lead line, you will learn how to make your pony walk and halt. This is not as easy as it sounds. The aim is to make the pony walk purposefully and with energy and to halt when you tell it to do so. The pony should be balanced, alert, and responsive to your aids at all times.

Square halt

To achieve a square halt, sit deep in the saddle with the horse's front and hind legs in line. Lean your weight backward slightly, and gently hold back on the reins. The pony is standing still, but it should be full of contained energy, ready to set off again.

Not listening

Some ponies ignore their rider's aids. Riders do not always give strong enough aids for their ponies, which then plod along sleepily with their noses stuck out. Applying the legs more strongly and shortening the reins will improve the pony's gaits.

Keep a contact
Although you have stopped, keep your legs against the pony's sides, and keep hold of the reins.

Hind legs
A gentle nudge with your own leg will make the pony move its hind leg on that side into line.

Front legs
As you ride forward into halt try to make sure that the front legs are in line.

Working on the bit

When you are riding a horse or pony it should always be "on the bit." This means that its head is held vertically and its mouth is below the level of the rider's hands. In this position the rider has the best possible control over the horse. It can be difficult to achieve and maintain, especially for an inexperienced rider and a pony that may not be perfectly schooled, but you can do it with practice.

Balanced
The pony is well balanced and ready to walk on again when you ask it to do so.

Head position
The pony is holding its head just behind the vertical, but it is striding out well.

Walk to halt and halt to walk

This is achieved by pressure from your legs and on the reins and shifting your weight in your seat. Although your lower legs and your hands—via the reins—should always be in contact with the pony, increasing or decreasing that contact tells it what you want it to do. Once the pony has obeyed your aids, relax them.

1 To ask a pony to walk, sit up straight, and "feel" the pony's mouth by gently tightening the reins. Move your weight forward, and squeeze its sides with your lower legs behind the girth.

3 Try to get the pony to halt squarely. Although you have stopped do not completely relax your position. Maintain contact with your legs and hands to keep the pony alert.

2 To halt, sit down deep in the saddle, and lean your weight backward slightly. To stop the pony from moving forward, resist the movement with your hands and the reins.

4 To move off into a walk again, press your legs more firmly into the pony's sides, and relax the reins a little to let it walk forward. Then relax your aids, but maintain contact.

Turning left and right

When you are turning a pony, your outside leg and inside hand—that is your right leg and left hand if you are turning left—produce the movement. They are supported by the inside leg, which keeps the pony steady; and the outside hand, which reinforces the inside hand. The pony should not wander forward while turning.

Your left hand moves back toward the pony's saddle.

View from above

When you look down on a pony and its rider as they turn, you can see how much the pony's body bends around the rider's inside leg. The rider's body shifts as it follows the pony's, and their head turns so that it faces the way they are going.

The left rein is gently pulled back to turn the pony's head.

Your right leg starts the movement with pressure behind the girth.

Your right hand is held close to the pony's neck.

The right rein supports the left rein by pressing against the neck.

The pony's bit is pulled to the left by the left rein.

1 Starting from a halt, press your right leg into the pony's side behind the girth, and gently pull your left rein back.

Turning left

When you are turning left, the pony's front legs and right hind leg move around its left hind leg. As soon as you have completed the turn you should drive the pony forward to a walk or trot in a straight line.

2 Keep your left leg near the girth. Bring the right rein over to press on the pony's neck.

3 As it starts to turn the pony's front legs move in a semicircle around its hind legs.

4 Continue to apply your hand and leg aids until you have turned the pony as far as you want to go.

1 Begin by pressing your left leg against the pony's side just behind the girth.

Turning right

In a turn to the right the pony's front legs and left hind leg move around its right hind leg. Its neck and spine bend in the direction of the movement.

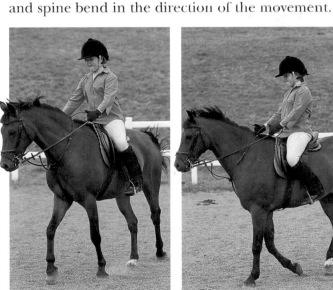

2 Feel the right rein to turn the pony's head by bringing your hand back slightly.

3 Move your left hand toward the right to press the left rein against the pony's neck.

4 Continue to drive the pony around with your left leg. Try not to let it step forward as it turns.

Practicing a posting trot

Before you learn to trot practice posting with the horse standing still. Take your weight on your feet in the stirrups, stand for a moment, and then sit down again. If you feel unsteady, rest your hands on the front of the saddle or on the horse's withers.

Stand up in the stirrups, keeping your knees slightly bent and taking your weight on the balls of your feet.

Lower yourself gently down to sit back in the saddle again. Do not let yourself flop down with a bump.

Learning to trot

The trot is a two-beat gait in which the pony's legs move in diagonal pairs: left fore and right hind, right fore and left hind. Because of this, it is very bumpy for the rider. To even out the bumps you post, or rise to the trot, most of the time. But for more advanced riding you also have to learn to sit to the trot. This is more difficult to do.

Posting trot

To post you take your weight off the saddle by standing in the stirrups as one pair of the pony's legs moves forward. Then sit down again as the opposite pair of legs moves. Try not to rise too high. At first it is difficult to get the rhythm right.

Changing the diagonal

When you post, you are said to be riding on either the right or the left diagonal, according to which pair of the pony's feet touches the ground as you sit in the saddle. To change the diagonal, you simply sit for an extra beat and then continue posting again. You should change the diagonal when you change the rein and alternate when outside of the arena.

On the left diagonal the rider sits in the saddle as the pony's left forefoot and right hind foot hit the ground. Most people ride on the left diagonal when they are trotting a circle to the right.

On the right diagonal the rider sits in the saddle as the pony's right forefoot and left hind foot hit the ground. Most people ride on the right diagonal when they are trotting a circle to the left.

Sitting trot

To sit to the trot, you must keep your seat and your thighs in contact with the saddle all the time and not bump around. You need good balance to do this, and you must relax the lower part of your back and allow it to absorb the pony's movements.

Transitions

A change of gait is called a transition. Going faster is an upward transition, going more slowly is a downward transition. To carry out transitions successfully you need impulsion, which is the energy you create in the pony by using the aids.

From walk . . .
Start with a good walk with the pony striding forward full of energy. To ask for trot, shorten your reins, squeeze with your legs behind the girth, and push with your seat. As the pony moves forward into a trot, ease your aids.

. . . to trot
As the pony starts to trot relax your reins a little to allow it to move forward, but maintain contact. If it seems to want to go back to walk, you will need to reapply your legs to keep it going. If necessary, use a crop.

Trotting
Once the pony gets into its stride you need to keep it trotting with a good, even rhythm. Keep contact with your hands and legs. How strong this contact must be will depend on how forward-going the pony is.

From trot . . .
To carry out a downward transition from trot to walk, sit deep in the saddle and squeeze with your legs behind the girth to drive the pony forward into its bit. At the same time, resist the forward movement with your hands.

. . . back to walk
When the pony slows down to walk, relax your aids, but still maintain contact with your legs and hands. You may still need to drive it forward to get a good, free-striding walk, and you still need to maintain impulsion.

Cantering

The canter is a wonderful gait once you have learned how to sit to it. At first you will bump out of the saddle, which is uncomfortable. To sit to the canter, you must keep in contact with the saddle, and at the same time try and relax.

The aids

To canter on the right lead, squeeze with your left leg behind the girth and tighten your right rein. Keep your right leg pressed into the pony on the girth. Reverse the aids in order to canter on the left lead.

Keep your back straight.

Sit deep in the saddle.

Left leg gives aid for canter right.

Tips for cantering

Before you give the aids to canter the pony has to be going forward well and be balanced. This will be in trot when you are learning. You must drive the pony forward with your legs and control the energy with your hands—do not let it trot faster and faster and become unbalanced.

Try to relax the lower part of your back when you canter so you can follow the pony's movements.

Do not lean forward out of the saddle because the pony may interpret this as a signal to go faster.

Keep your reins fairly short, and maintain contact with the pony's mouth so it cannot get its head down.

The pony should be light on its feet when it is cantering.

The gait

A canter is a three-beat gait in which the horse's front and hind legs on one side are farther forward than those on the other. The horse is said to be leading with, or on, the right or the left leg. When it is on the right leg, its feet hit the ground in the following sequence: left hind, right hind and left front together, right front. After this there is a moment of suspension when all the feet are off the ground at the same time. A well-schooled horse can change lead in the air. This is called a flying change.

Good working canter

The working canter is the gait you will learn when you first start cantering. Traveling at average speed, the pony should move freely with good rhythm and respond to your aids at all times.

Keep a good contact on the reins so that you stay in control.

Keep the pony cantering with pressure from your right leg.

This pony is cantering with its right leg leading.

The pony's weight is on its left front leg and right hind leg.

Checking the lead

You should be able to feel which leg is leading while cantering because the pony's shoulder on that side will be slightly farther forward than its other shoulder. But when you are first learning, you may need to take a quick look down to check.

The ears laid back show that the pony is unhappy.

You are thrown off balance.

Your seat is thrown out of the saddle.

The right hind leg leads.

The left foreleg leads.

Cross cantering

When a pony leads with one front leg and the opposite hind leg while cantering, it is said to be cross cantering. It is uncomfortable for both the pony and the rider. If it happens, go back to a trot and give the aids to canter again.

Right fore leading
The right hind and left fore are just hitting the ground.

Right fore leading
All the pony's weight is now put on the right foreleg.

In the air
For a brief moment all the pony's legs are in the air.

Riding at top speed

Galloping is very exciting for both pony and rider. Do not attempt it until you are sure you can control your pony at a canter. Choose a good place to gallop. A smooth field with an uphill slope is ideal—it is easier to stop when going uphill! Never gallop over rough ground, near or up to other ponies, or in a confined space. Make sure there is plenty of room to maneuver.

Half seat position

When you gallop, you should go into a half seat position, or galloping position. This means leaning forward and placing your weight on your knees and feet. Raise your rear just clear of the saddle, but keep your balance. Practice the position while stationary.

Asking for a gallop

Get your pony into a good canter, and get into a half seat position. Urge your pony forward with your legs until you are going fast enough for the canter to become a gallop. Keep contact with its mouth through the reins.

The gallop

The gallop is the fastest gait. It is a four-beat gait, with each hoof hitting the ground separately. When the left front leg is leading, the sequence is right hind, left hind, right front, and then left front.

Slowing down

Ponies love to gallop, and they can be difficult to stop. When you want to slow down to a canter, maintain contact with your legs and sit back in the saddle, taking an upright position again. Resist the forward movement with the reins until the pony slows down.

Body position
When you are in a half seat position, keep your head up, and look where you are going.

Suspension
There is a moment in a gallop when all four hooves are off the ground.

Fast forward

The average pony gallops at around 15 mph (24km/h). This may not sound fast, but when you are thundering along with the wind whistling past your ears, it feels it! The Thoroughbred is the fastest horse in the world. It gallops about 30 mph (50km/h), but its record race speed is an amazing 43 mph (69.2km/h) over a quarter of a mile.

Seat position
Sit down in the deepest part of the saddle with your ear, shoulder, hip, and heel aligned. Keep your heels down.

How to hold the reins
Separate the reins with your index finger, and hold them above and in front of the saddle's horn.

Leg position
Ride with a nearly straight leg and a fairly long stirrup, letting your legs hang down lightly by the horse's sides.

Western riding

When riding western, you use only the lightest of touches to tell the horse what to do. When it has obeyed your aids and is carrying out your wishes, you sit still and do nothing. You do not need to keep in contact with its mouth, but hold the reins very lightly, except when giving specific aids. You can use your voice as an aid to tell it to change gaits and to halt.

Legs, seat, and hands

You should sit up tall and straight in the saddle, yet be in a relaxed position. Rest the balls of your feet in the stirrups. You hold your hands higher than you would in English-style riding, at approximately the level of your elbows. When you are riding western, you may hold the reins in one hand or two, except in competitions.

Turning left

Giving the aids for turning with the reins in one hand only is called neck-reining. The rein on the inside of the turn makes the horse look in the direction it is going. The rein on the outside puts pressure on its neck, telling it to move over.

1 Move your right hand to the left, so the left rein turns the horse's head in the correct direction and the right rein presses against its neck.

2 Look in the direction in which you want to go. At the same time relax your left leg and push the horse over to the left with your right leg.

A group lesson
In a group lesson you have to keep up with the pace of the pony in front of you and keep your pony's mind on its work.

Passing shoulder to shoulder

While you are riding in the school you may have to ride past another pony and rider. When you do this, you should pass left shoulder to left shoulder. This is also the generally accepted way of passing another rider you may meet when on a trail ride.

Riding at the correct distance

When you are riding in a group you must leave a pony's length between your pony and the pony in front of you. Riding close behind another pony may upset it, and it might kick out at your own pony and injure it or you.

Riding in a group

Riding in a group can be a challenge at first. There are many things to remember. You must control your own pony, but at the same time consider what other riders are doing. Your pony may behave differently, too, in the company of others. It may be more excitable or it may refuse to leave the other ponies to carry out your wishes. You will learn both from your own riding and from watching others.

Exercises in the arena

Carrying out individual exercises in the arena that involve changes of gait and direction, such as riding circles and loops, is a good way of testing your riding ability. You have to manage your pony and give the correct aids at the right time. Your instructor will help you if you need assistance.

Riding exercises in pairs

If you have four or more riders in your group, you can carry out exercises in pairs. This is fun to do, and it is also a great test of timing and judgment. You have to be level with each other all the time, which is difficult if one pony has a longer stride than the other. You might ride up the arena, circle in opposite directions, then pair up again. With practice you can do this at a trot and a canter.

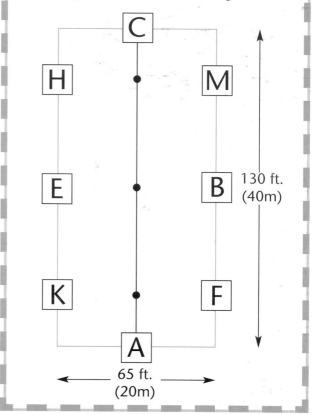

Dressage arena

Most arenas are marked out with letters like a dressage arena. You can use the letters as points at which to change your direction or gait. For example, you might walk from K to H, trot to F, and so on. To remember the sequence of the letters, use a phrase like "All King Edward's Horses Can Make Big Fences."

C
H   M
E   B   130 ft. (40m)
K   F
A

65 ft. (20m)

Changing gaits

If you are told to walk to H and then trot to M, you should break into a trot as your pony's shoulder becomes level with the letter. It is a challenge, and your pony must be well balanced and obedient to your aids. You have to judge exactly the right moment to give the aids, and you have to deliver them precisely. This takes a lot of practice.

Figures to ride

The top row of figures shows ways of changing the rein—altering the direction in which you are riding around the arena. Some of the other figures also involve a change of rein. The aim is to make all these shapes as accurate as possible. A circle should be round, not flattened. A figure eight should be made up of two equal circles. The loops of a serpentine should also be of equal size.

Ride up the center from the right rein, and then turn left to change the rein.

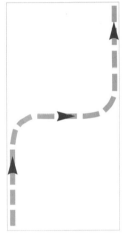

Ride across the center of the arena, and then turn left to change the rein.

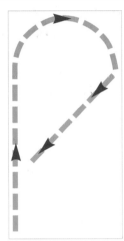

Ride across a short diagonal, such as from M to E or from corner to corner.

Riding a two-loop serpentine across the center is another way of changing the rein.

A 16 ft. (5m) loop is a curve that goes up to 16 ft. (5m) in from the long side of the school.

You can ride circles of 30 and 60 ft. (10 and 20m) in diameter from a number of points.

Riding a figure eight's two complete circles involves two changes of rein.

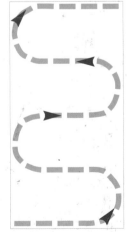

Riding a three-loop serpentine leaves you going in the same direction as you started.

Riding a four-loop serpentine means you end up going around in the opposite direction.

Without stirrups and reins

O nce you have had a few riding lessons you may be asked to ride without stirrups and later without reins. Riding without stirrups is an excellent way of improving your seat in the saddle. Riding without reins improves your balance. You should never rely on the reins to keep your balance.

Whole ride no stirrups

When you have riding lessons, you may spend part of each session riding without stirrups. To stop them from banging against the pony's sides, you cross them over in front of the saddle. The group may walk or trot around together, or you may take turns to trot around while the rest of the group walks.

Lungeing without reins

When riding without reins, you should tie them in a knot in front of the horse's withers to stop them from hanging loose. When you are on a lunge line, you do not have to worry about steering or stopping the horse, although you will learn to change direction using your legs.

Walk on the lunge
You can concentrate on your position in the saddle and use the leg aids to control the horse's pace and direction.

Trot on the lunge
You may feel insecure when trotting. If so, hold on to the front of the saddle or a neck strap with one or both hands.

Without stirrups

Let your legs hang down beside the pony. Keep them pressed against its sides with your heels down and your toes up.

Try to sit deep down in the saddle and not bump out of it.

Relax your back so you can follow the pony's movements.

Riding without stirrups is hard work on your muscles, and your legs will ache afterward.

Holding on to the saddle

When you first ride without stirrups, you will probably hold on to the front of the saddle with one hand while you hold the reins with the other. Your instructor may take you on a lead line or on the lunge until you become more experienced.

The instructor will lead your pony very slowly at first to let you get used to being without stirrups.

Sit up straight as if you had stirrups.

If you hold both reins in one hand, keep it in the correct position.

Without reins

Riding without reins is a test of balance. An experienced rider should be able to ride independently of the reins.

Using your leg aids, practice turning the pony right and left.

If you lose your balance, hold the saddle or neck strap.

If your pony misbehaves or tries to run off, take hold of the reins immediately.

Trot on your own

When you have become more experienced at riding without stirrups, you will be allowed to ride on your own. You can walk, trot, canter, and even jump without stirrups. You will need to use both hands on the reins, but if you feel unsafe, you could rest your hands, still holding the reins, on the front of the saddle. You have to keep contact with the pony's mouth.

Forward and back

Keep your seat in the saddle with your legs in the correct position. Then lean forward to touch the horse's head behind its ears or as far as you can reach. Go back to your starting position, and then lean back to touch the top of the horse's tail, twisting at the waist as you do so. Do not pull on the horse's mouth.

Around the world

In this exercise you go around in a complete circle while sitting on the horse. As you move around steady yourself by holding on to the saddle.

Exercises in the saddle

Doing stretching and twisting exercises on your pony is fun. They will help make you supple, and once you have had a bit of practice doing them you will become a more confident rider. Start all the exercises by sitting in the correct position in the saddle (pages 154–155). Only practice the exercises when you have someone with you who can hold your pony.

1 Tie your reins in a knot on the horse's neck, and take both your feet out of the stirrups.

2 Lift your right leg over the horse's neck—be careful not to kick it as you do so.

3 Swing your left leg over the quarters. Hold the saddle with your right hand.

4 You are now facing backward. It feels strange without the horse's neck in front!

5 Start going back by twisting around and swinging your right leg over the horse's back.

6 Hold on to the front and the back of the saddle as you sit on the horse facing sideways.

7 Shift yourself around in the saddle as you prepare to move your left leg back over again.

8 Swing your left leg back over the horse's neck to return to where you started.

Arm exercises

Stretch your arms high up in the air, and then rest your hands on your shoulders. Stretch both your arms out to the sides, and bring your hands back to your shoulders. Reach forward, and then go back again.

Leg stretching

Sit in the correct position in the saddle, and keep the upper part of your legs still. Swing your left leg forward as far as you can, moving it from the knee down. Then swing it back as far as you can. Repeat the exercise with your right leg. Now bring both legs back to the usual position. Moving one at a time, point your feet down as far as they will go and then up to stretch your ankles.

Leaning back

You may need to hold on to the front of the saddle to do this exercise but try to manage without doing so. Simply lean right back until your head is resting on the pony's quarters. Stay there for a moment or two, and then sit up again. This is a good way of developing the strong stomach muscles you need for riding.

Touching toes

Lift your right hand up in the air, and then bend down over the left side of your saddle and touch your left toe. Straighten up again and repeat the exercise, lifting your left hand up and bending down to touch your right toe.

Looking
forward

Once you have learned to ride you can enjoy many activities. You might join a pony club or go away to a riding camp. You can go on trail rides with friends and take part in horse shows and gymkhanas.

Hand signals on the road

Give clear signals to pedestrians and cyclists as well as drivers, leaving plenty of time before you carry out your intended movement. Hold your reins firmly in the other hand to keep control of your pony.

Turning right
When you wish to turn right, first check behind you that no vehicle is approaching. Hold your right arm out straight to give the signal. Check that it is safe to turn before you do so.

Turning left
To turn left, check for approaching vehicles, and then hold your left arm out straight to give the signal. Before you make the turn check again that it is safe for you to do so.

Riding safely on the road

Always ride on the correct side of the road, and keep to the inside. Never ride more than two abreast, and stick to single file on narrow lanes. If you are riding two abreast, then the rider on the inside of a turn to the left or right should make the hand signal.

Road safety

Before you ride on the road learn the systems of rules and signals that apply. If possible, take a road safety test. Make sure you can control your pony in all situations. Avoid riding on main roads and narrow roads that do not have grass shoulders. Never ride on the road at night or when it is foggy.

Thank you
To thank a driver who slows down for you, raise a hand and smile. If you do not wish to take a hand off the reins, nod your head and smile at the driver.

Stop
If you wish to ask another road user to stop, hold up your right hand in front of you. Do not be afraid of asking drivers to stop or slow down if necessary.

 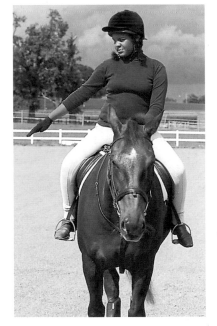

Asking traffic to slow down
To ask a driver to slow down, hold your outside arm out to the side and move it slowly up and down. Thank them when they do slow down.

Light-reflective equipment

You should never ride on a road at night, but on gray, winter afternoons you can wear light-reflecting safety gear. You can buy a reflective belt, hat cover, and vest for yourself as well as a bridle cover, leg bands, tail guard, and exercise sheet for your pony. You can also buy lights that clip to your stirrups, showing a white light at the front and red at the back.

Safety vest

A safety vest is worn over your outdoor clothes. It may have a light-reflective strip across the back and front, or it may feature a warning to other road users such as "Caution: horse and rider" or "Please pass wide and slow."

Reflective strip

Safety vest

Trail riding

Trail riding—riding ouside of the arena—with friends is fun. If you plan your route beforehand, you can make the ride more interesting. You might explore woods and meadows—using fallen logs as jumps—canter along a trail, or even ford a shallow stream. Tell an adult where you are going and when you expect to return.

Riding across open ground

It is fun to canter or gallop across open ground if you are allowed to, but make sure that you can control your pony before you start. Go uphill if possible, and stay at least a pony's length away from other horses.

Opening and closing gates

A gate on a trail should have a latch that you can reach when mounted. You should then be able to open the gate, walk through it, and close it without dismounting. Practice at the stable before you try it on a trail.

1 Ride right up to the gate and position your pony alongside it so you can reach out to work the latch.

2 Lean forward to release the latch. Keep your pony standing still with the reins in your other hand.

3 Push the gate open, and hold on to it while you ride through. Do not let it swing back on your pony.

4 Once through the gate, turn your pony around and close it again. Make sure the gate is securely shut.

Riding on trails

In some areas you may be able to use trails specifically designed for horseback riders. When riding on one of these trails, follow the signposts and do not stray from the track if it crosses a meadow. Watch out for farm animals, and make sure that any gates you may go through are closed and properly secured.

Riding past other animals

You may ride past a pasture in which other horses, or cattle, charge and upset your pony. Try to keep your pony calm. Keep your reins short, and use your legs strongly to ride past them.

Riding a pony through water

Only cross a stream if you know the water is shallow. Many ponies are nervous of water unless they know that there is firm ground beneath it. Let the pony take its time at first, but then drive it on firmly with your legs and seat.

Your first jumping lessons

Approach
The approach to a jump is very important. You must drive the pony firmly forward with pressure from your legs.

Learning to jump is very exciting. There is a lot to learn, but if you ride correctly over trotting poles and small fences, in time big fences will not be a problem. The pony must be moving with impulsion before takeoff, and you have to follow its movement over the jump.

Jumping position

For jumping you need to learn the jumping position. When jumping, shorten the stirrups a hole or two. Lift your bottom clear of the saddle and lean forward, putting your weight on your knees and on your feet in the stirrups.

Leading over poles

First jumping lessons for both ponies and riders are usually over poles laid on the ground and spaced out so the pony can walk and trot over them. To begin with, your instructor may lead your pony over them.

The half-seat position

You use the half-seat position when galloping to take the weight off the horse's back. Shorten your reins, and keep your knees pressed into the saddle and your heels down. If your heels come up, you will lose your balance.

1 As you approach the poles shorten your reins slightly and get into jumping position. Drive the pony on with your legs. Keep heels down and your head up, and look ahead to where you are going.

2 The pony will lift up its feet to trot over the poles. It should move smoothly and evenly with a regular rhythm and not jump over the poles. Use a posting trot when you are trotting over poles.

Keep your legs in contact
with the pony's sides and your heels down during the jump. Feel the reins, but do not pull.

Takeoff
When the pony's hind legs propel it into the air, lean forward to go with the pony's movement. Let your hands follow its head.

Trotting over poles

Trotting over poles is a good exercise for a pony. Lay three or four poles 3–3.5 ft. (1–1.3m) apart, according to the pony's size. When the spacing is correct, the pony's hind foot will hit the ground halfway between two of the poles.

1 Walk over the poles at first. Go around the arena, and try approaching them from both directions. Use jumping position as you ride over the poles.

2 When you are happy in walk, trot around the arena, and as you go around concentrate on the row of poles. Keep a good rhythm in the trot, and look ahead as you ride—not at the poles.

Sequence of a jump

A jump can be divided into four parts: the approach, takeoff, suspension in the air, and landing. You can approach a jump in a trot or a canter—both must be balanced and rhythmical. The takeoff has to be at the right distance for the horse to clear the fence. Once the pony has landed, do not hesitate. Ride it straight on toward the next fence.

Your first jump

After trotting poles, you will learn to take your first jump. It will not be very high. Crossed poles encourage the pony to jump in the center, where the fence is lower. Wings placed at each side of a jump help prevent the pony from avoiding it and running out. This counts as a refusal in competitions.

Landing
When the pony lands, keep the forward position and make sure you do not pull on its mouth.

Getting larger

Once you are confident jumping a low rail, you can try something more ambitious. A good way to progress is to keep the fences low, but make them wider. A wide fence, called a spread, makes your pony stretch out further to clear it.

Top-class jumping

To clear huge fences like this, the horse has to stretch its head and neck right out.

Jumping higher

If you want to do really well at show jumping, you need to spend a lot of time practicing with your pony. You will need to train on the flat as well as practice over fences. Flat work is important because your pony needs to be supple and obedient to jump well. It must listen to your commands so it does not rush the fences or take off at the wrong moment. When you are jumping, whether for practice or in the ring, you should push your pony with your seat and legs so it knows for certain what you want it to do.

Seeing a distance

Three or four strides before a fence, try to judge how many strides your pony needs before takeoff. This is called "seeing a distance." If a pony is too near a fence, it will not be able to jump. Too far away, it may knock down a pole.

Water jump

A water jump is a wide pool of water with a low fence on the takeoff side. The horse has to stretch out to jump over the obstacle without putting a foot in it.

Double combination

Four fence combination

Combination

Two or more fences close together count as one obstacle, called a combination. If a horse refuses at one part, it has to jump the whole sequence again. The number of strides between fences in a combination can vary.

Simple dressage

Once you have learned to control your pony and you are confident doing basic gaits in the ring, you may progress to more advanced riding and simple dressage movements, called training on the flat. Even if you do not go on to enter any competitions, careful training will help you learn to communicate with your pony and get the most from it.

On the bit

When the pony is balanced between your hands and legs and you have soft contact with the bit, it is "on the bit." It will hold its head straight, with its mouth lower than your hands. This position allows maximum control and feeling of your pony's motion.

Square halt

With practice you will be able to do a square halt where the front and back hooves are perfectly in line with each other. Your weight must be distributed evenly so your pony stays balanced.

Turning on the forehand

The horse's hindlegs move around its inside foreleg. To turn to the right, tighten the right rein, bring the left rein over in support, press with your left leg, and hold the hindquarters steady with your right leg.

Shoulder-in
The horse's front legs follow an inner track. It crosses its front legs as it travels, but its hind legs move straight forward.

Lateral work

Lateral means "sideways." In lateral work, the horse's body forms a curve, so its front legs move on a different track from its hind legs. For this reason, lateral work is also known as "work on two tracks."

Travers
The horse's hind legs follow an inner track. Its body is bent to the outside of the ring.

Leg yield
The horse moves forward and sideways away from the rider's leg. Its body is straight.

Riding sidesaddle

To ride sidesaddle, you face front, with your right leg over a pommel called the fixed head. Your left leg rests under another pommel—the leaping head. It is supported by a single stirrup. The saddle is secured by a girth and a balance strap. A pony has special training to carry a sidesaddle and responds to a whip on the right side instead of the rider's leg.

Counter canter

Horses and ponies normally lead with their inside leg when they canter, but for a movement called the counter canter, they need to lead with their outside leg. This is difficult to perform, and the horse needs to be well balanced.

Advanced riding

If you watch a top-class dressage partnership, the horse seems to carry out perfect movements effortlessly, and the rider gives no visible aids. However, it will take lots of practice before you will be able to carry out such advanced dressage gaits and movements properly. Even the best riders were not born champions. They have spent many years working hard and patiently.

The art of riding

Spanish School

The classical art of riding is practiced by the Spanish Riding School of Vienna in Austria and the Cadre Noir of Saumur in France. Riders at these schools perform complicated steps based on the horse's natural movements. This horse is performing a levade—a controlled half rear.

Turn on the haunches

This is when a horse pivots around its inside hind leg, which should remain still. It uses its other legs in the same sequence as it does when going forward.

Collection and extension

To "collect" a horse is to shorten its frame, making it push off its haunches. Its stride is shorter and more bouncy, and the gait is slower. Extension is the opposite. The horse stretches out its head and neck, and it takes longer, lower strides, increasing its speed.

Collected to extended walk
As the horse moves from a collected walk, through a medium walk, into an extended walk, it gradually lengthens its stride and stretches out its head and neck.

Collected walk

Collected trot
The horse moves at a steady, collected gait, but still with energy. Its head and neck are raised and its hindquarters appear lower.

Extended trot
The horse is moving much faster, with a longer stride. As it extends the trot, it flicks its front hooves forward.

Flying change

When a horse changes its lead while cantering, when all its feet are off the ground, it is called a "flying change." It is a difficult movement to perform. An experienced horse and rider may do a flying change every stride.

Half-pass

This is a lateral movement in which the horse moves forward and sideways at the same time. It crosses its outside legs over, in front of the inside legs, bending its head in the direction in which it is going. This horse (right) is moving to the left.

In the air
This horse has changed lead in the air and is now on a right lead.

Collected/medium walk

Medium walk

Extended walk

Free walk on a long rein

Collected canter
The collected canter is a slow, rocking gait. The horse must be supple and relaxed. The rider should sit deep in the saddle and follow the movement.

Extended canter
The horse stretches its neck and lengthens its stride to cover as much ground as possible. Its weight, and that of the rider, move forward.

Taking part in events

Y ou may simply enjoy pleasure riding, but if you want to compete, there are a variety of activities in which you can take part. You may want to join a Pony Club or a local chapter of the 4-H club. You can enter showing, jumping, and gymkhana competitions at local shows, and you might like to try dressage or hunter paces.

Riding clubs
Local riding clubs hold all kinds of events. If you become a member, you can take part and also find out about other equestrian activities going on in your area.

Endurance riding

If you take part in a long-distance endurance ride, you and your pony will need to be very fit. You may have to cover up to 50 miles (80km) a day. Arabian horses have good stamina and excel at this sport.

Vaulting

Vaulting is gymnastics on horseback and requires great athletic ability as well as riding skills. You can take part on your own or as part of a team, performing leaps and balancing feats with the horse on a lunge rein.

Braiding the mane

1 Dampen the mane, then, starting at the poll, divide it into same-size sections. Hold them in place with a rubber band tied loosely at the base.

2 Remove the rubber band, and tightly braid each section. Tie with rubber bands. Tie yarn over the rubber bands, leaving long ends.

3 Thread the yarn through a large needle and pull the ends up through the top of the braid, making a loop.

4 Roll up the braid by folding it in half again. Hold it in place by tying the yarn around it and knotting it. Cut off any excess yarn.

Getting ready for a show

Getting ready for a show is fun, but it is hard work and takes time to do it right. If the weather is warm, you can give your pony a bath, but if it is cold, just sponge your pony off. You must also groom your pony thoroughly. If you are braiding its mane and tail, do not wash them. It is difficult to braid a clean mane. You must make sure the tack is clean, too, so your pony will look its best.

Bands or sewn?
You can secure your pony's braids with special rubber bands made specifically for this purpose—they are tiny and available in different coat colors.

Making the most of your pony

Quarter marks

Make quarter marks on your pony's hindquarters by wetting the coat and brushing it in different angles. You can also use special stencils to make squares or diamonds. Use hairspray to make the marks last longer.

Make white tails and markings whiter by rubbing in cornstarch.

Trim hairy fetlocks and hairs under the jaw and on the muzzle.

Pull the mane after the pony has been exercised, when its skin

Pulling a mane

pores are open. Use a pulling comb to separate 3–4 long hairs from underneath, wrap them around the comb, then pull.

Hairdressing
If you end up with a few wisps of hair sticking out of the braids, use hair gel to smooth them down flat.

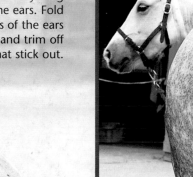

Braiding the forelock

Dampen the forelock and braid it in the same way as you have braided the mane, using the yarn to secure it in place. To reverse the braid, cross the strands of hair underneath, instead of over the top.

Trimming
Carefully trim any long hairs in the ears. Fold the sides of the ears together and trim off the hairs that stick out.

Braiding tips

You should give your pony an even number of braids, including the forelock. Depending on its size, it may have seven, nine, or eleven braids on its neck. A lot of braids make a short neck look longer. Fewer, thicker braids make a long neck look shorter. If you are good at braiding, you can make the braids stick up or lie flat to make the neck look wider or narrower.

Baby oil
Wipe a little baby oil or petroleum jelly around the muzzle of a dark-skinned pony to make it look clean and shiny.

Braiding the tail

Take long hairs from each side of the dock and braid them with hair from the center until you reach the end of the tailbone, then continue braiding without taking hair from the sides. Tie off the braid, fold it under, and secure with yarn.

Going to a show

Competing in a show is fun. After all the preparation, it is exciting to ride around the ring, looking your best and trying your hardest. In between classes, do not tear around, but let your pony rest in the shade. Give it a drink and some hay, or let it graze. It is great to win a ribbon, but do not blame your pony or get upset if you do not do it this time. There is always next time.

Unloading backward
If your pony needs to back out of a trailer, stand at its head and push it gently backward. Ask someone to stand by the ramp to guide it.

Unloading safely

Untie your pony before you take down the butt bar or butt chain. Lead it out forward if you can. When you go down the ramp, do not rush your pony. Some ramps are slippery and steep, and your pony could hurt itself if it goes too fast. Ask two friends to stand on either side of the ramp if you think your pony might try to jump off sideways.

Unloading forward
If the trailer has a side ramp, you can lead your pony out forward— you may have to lead it from the right side. Do not let it pull you.

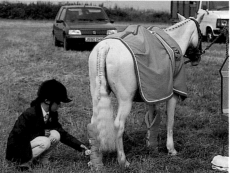

First things first
Tie up your pony, or ask someone to hold it while you take off its boots. Check it all over to see that it is all right after the journey.

Ready to jump
If you are entering a jumping event, it is a good idea to wear a body protector that meets safety standards.

Ready to show
Look as professional as you can for a showing class. It will give you confidence if you look your best.

Waiting safely

Leave your pony tied to a trailer only if you know it will not get upset. Fasten its lead rope to a piece of string so it can break free if it panics. Your pony will probably wait patiently if you hang up some hay for it.

The secretary

When you arrive at the show grounds, check in at the show secretary's tent or trailer. You can collect your number here and enter classes if you have not already done so. You can also find the results of classes here. The secretary will post them up on a noticeboard.

Sharing a pony

If you are sharing a pony with a friend, make sure you agree in advance which classes you will enter. It is fun to watch each other and help prepare for the classes. But do not ask your pony to do too much and exhaust it.

Fun and games

Gymkhanas and shows have all kinds of mounted games and races to try. Some are for teams, some for individuals. You need to be good at mounted games, be able to think and act quickly, and have an obedient and fast-moving pony. If you belong to a Pony Club, you could become a member of the mounted games team and compete around the country.

Flag relay
This is a team game in which you have to gallop to a flag, lean over, and pick it up, then gallop back and hand it on to the next member of your team.

Handy tips

You need to be quick, fit, and athletic to do really well in mounted games.

Your pony must be fast, agile, and, above all, obedient—it is no use asking it to gallop if you cannot get it to stop or turn.

Barrel racing
A pony that can gallop and turn quickly without losing its balance is a great help in this type of bending race.

Practice makes perfect

No matter what games you enter, you need to practice for them. Training your pony until it responds to all your commands will make a big difference in competition. Practice going from a halt to a canter to a gallop, and changing gaits and direction at full speed. See how quickly you can mount and dismount, and learn how to vault on and off. You can also get used to leaning out of the saddle to pick things up.

Vaulting on

Being able to vault onto your pony while it is moving saves a lot of time in games and races. It is easier if your pony is small and you have long legs! You have to run with your pony, holding the saddle, then spring up and swing yourself over.

Egg and spoon
You need a steady hand for this. The eggs are not real, but you still have to keep one on the spoon!

Tire race
You and a partner have to leap off your ponies, climb through a tire, and then get back on again.

Make a tower
You have to lean right out of the saddle to stack the plastic tubs without unbalancing your pony.

Potato race
Having picked up a potato and raced down the field, you then have to throw it into a bucket.

Show jumping classes

Show jumping is a popular riding sport. Most classes have a time limit, some are against the clock, where the fastest round with the least faults wins. You are penalized if your horse knocks down a fence, refuses a jump, runs out, or if you fall off. Three refusals or taking the wrong course means you are eliminated. If more than one person jumps a clean round, there is a "jump off." This means you will have to ride a shorter, timed course to decide the winner.

Walking the course

Before a show jumping class, all the competitors have a chance to walk the course. This gives you time to plan and memorize the route you will take. You can also look carefully at each jump and judge how many strides your pony will need to take between combination fences.

In the warm-up arena

The warm-up arena is an area, usually with one or two practice jumps, where you can warm up your pony before its class. Once the class has started, you will have to wait near the entrance to the ring for your number to be called.

Triple bars
Three bars, making a wide spread

Brush and rails
A spread highest in the center

Gate
A high, upright fence

Wall
Made of "bricks" that fall off easily

Filler
A solid part below the poles

Upright poles
Poles right above each other

Double oxer
Brush between two sets of poles

Hog's back
The highest pole is in the center

Types of jumps

Show jumps fall into four main categories: uprights, spreads, combinations, and water. Uprights are difficult for ponies to jump. Spread fences are easier because they are lower at the front. Combinations—jumps with only a stride or two between each fence—need good judgment from pony and rider. To clear water jumps, ponies have to stretch themselves out.

Thinking ahead

Throughout your round, it is important to keep a good position in the saddle. Drive your pony forward confidently as you jump, and look ahead to the next fence.

Saving time

It is important to memorize the course before you enter the ring so that as you land from each jump, you can be thinking about the next one. Against the clock, you can save precious seconds by taking the shortest route between fences.

Clean round

Do not rush around the ring—your pony will lose its balance and hit fences.

Push your pony firmly toward each fence. If it feels you hesitate, it may refuse.

If you feel your pony may refuse, give it a sharp tap with your crop behind the girth.

Do not hit your pony if it knocks a fence—just try to approach it better next time.

Showing and dressage tests

To compete in the show ring and dressage arena you need a well-trained horse or pony, and both of you must be clean and professional. In the show ring, a pony is judged on its conformation—its shape and proportions —its gaits, and its behavior. You will have to ride at a walk, trot, and canter on both reins; walk and trot your pony in hand; and sometimes do an individual show.

Showing in hand

When you are lined up in the ring, you will be asked to take off your pony's saddle so that the judge can inspect the pony. Then you will have to walk and trot your pony in hand so the judge can check that it moves straight.

Individual show

An individual show is a chance to show off your pony's gaits. Most people ride circles at trot and canter on both reins, or combine them to form a figure eight. At the end of your time, finish with a good, square halt.

Before the test

Before doing a dressage test, warm up a pony thoroughly to get it settled and working at its best. Some horses and ponies need more work than others, so give yourself plenty of time.

Riding the test

Concentrate and keep calm when riding in the dressage arena. The judges mark the test and write their comments on a score sheet. You will be given the sheet—it is a useful pointer to your strengths and weaknesses.

Dressage hints and tips

Check that your clothes and tack meet the requirements of the competition.

Make sure that you and your pony are immaculately clean and well groomed. It is important to make a good first impression on the judges.

Ask someone to call out each bit of the test as you practice, to help you remember it.

Make up rhymes to help you memorize the test.

Practice until you and your pony can carry out the test's requirements perfectly.

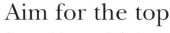
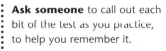

Aim for the top

Some riders and their horses specialize in dressage. This is Isabell Werth on Gigolo doing an extended trot at the World Equestrian Games in 1998. A great deal of training and effort lies behind the tests performed by top-class horses and riders.

Hedge

Ski jump

Log

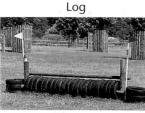
Tires

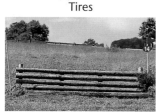
Rails

Cross-country

On a cross-country course, there are solid fences with long spaces in between. Both you and your pony need to be strong and brave. You will pick up penalty points for every mistake you make, such as refusing, jumping the wrong part of a fence, going the wrong way, falling off, or going over the time limit. The fences carry red and white flags. You must jump between them with the red on your right and the white on your left. You may have the choice between an easier, slower route or a faster, more difficult one.

Hunter paces

Cross-country jumping competitions are called hunter paces. There are paces for both horses and ponies. Courses often take you through fields and woodland, and you may have to open and close a gate. There is usually a set time in which you must try to finish one section or the whole course.

Types of fences

Cross-country fences are based on obstacles you might meet if you were riding through the countryside, such as rails, hedges, logs, walls, ditches, banks, and water. They are solid and do not give way if hit. They may be placed so that you have to jump them going up or down hills.

Walking the course

You are allowed to walk around a cross-country course before you ride it. This allows you to look at the fences and work out the best way to approach them. Check the ground on the approach and landing, and look out for things that might spook your pony, so that you are prepared.

Horse trials

In horse trials, you have to do dressage, cross-country, and show jumping. These are the supreme test of horse and rider. Precision and training is needed for the dressage; endurance, speed, and boldness for the cross-country; and suppleness and obedience for the show jumping. Experienced riders take part in events that last two or three days.

Steeplechase

Two- and three-day events include a steeplechase phase—about 12 fences over a distance of about 2.2 miles (3.6km). The course has to be ridden at around 25 mph (41km/h), which means a horse has to perform like a racehorse. At large events, competitors also have to ride along sections of roads and tracks, both before and after the steeplechase.

Training and driving

Breaking to harness

When a horse or pony has gotten used to wearing a harness and being long-reined, the traces can be attached to an old tire to get it used to dragging something along behind it. The trainer walks behind holding the long reins.

Long-reining off the bit

In this advanced form of long-reining the reins are attached to the horse's bit and pass through rings on the surcingle. The outside rein passes around the horse's quarters.

A horse's or pony's training begins when he or she is a very young foal. If they are handled with kindness, firmness, patience, and understanding, they will grow up to be confident and will learn to trust people. This trust forms the basis for all of their education. When they are three or four years old, the training will become more specialized, depending on whether they will be ridden, driven, or both. A few horses, through careful, patient teaching and a lot of practice, go on to become stars in their own specialist area—whether that is dressage, show jumping, eventing, police work, pulling a ceremonial carriage, or carrying a military band member.

Breaking in a horse

Teaching a horse or a pony to accept a rider and to understand the rider's signals, or "aids," is called "breaking in a horse" or "starting." The horse has to learn to wear a saddle and bridle and to have a bit in its mouth. Lungeing and long-reining help strengthen the muscles and make them supple.

Lunge cavesson and rein

A lunge cavesson has a padded noseband with three rings that are set on swivels.

Lungeing with side reins

Side reins, running from a snaffle bit to a surcingle, help adjust the horse's balance so that it can carry itself as if it had a rider. The reins also encourage it to make contact with the bit.

Lungeing with saddle

Once the horse has gotten used to the feel of a saddle on its back, it can be lunged wearing it, with the side reins in place. It is another step forward in the horse's education.

Lungeing a horse

When being lunged, a horse moves at a walk, trot, and canter in a circle around the trainer. At first an assistant leads the horse, but later the horse obeys its trainer's words of command.

Long-reining with side reins

Long-reining teaches the horse to change directions and pace through the use of the reins. The horse also learns how to balance and carry itself without the complication of the rider's weight.

Halter breaking

A foal is trained to wear a halter and to be led alongside its mother when it is only a few days old. Once it gets used to being led, one person can manage both the mare and foal.

Backing a young horse

Before sitting in the saddle for the first time the rider leans across it in order to accustom the horse to his or her weight.

Using a saddle

An alternative method of long-reining is to use a saddle and to pass the reins through the stirrup irons, with the leathers shortened so that the irons do not hit against the horse's sides.

First lessons

Once in the saddle—without stirrups in case he or she needs to dismount quickly—the rider sits very quietly on the horse while the trainer leads it around the arena.

How to drive a horse

When you are driving, you control a horse or a pony by using your voice, the reins, and the whip. "Walk on" and "trot on," said in an encouraging tone, tell the horse to move forward. "Whoa," said more slowly and reinforced with the reins, tells it to slow down or stop. A well-trained horse obeys the lightest of touches and commands.

Putting to

"Putting to" means attaching the vehicle to the horse's harness. The reins are looped over the horse's back. One person holds the horse, while another person brings up the vehicle and hooks the traces onto the trace hooks.

Fastening a tug

Tugs are leather loops that the ends of the shafts pass through. They are buckled to the back band, which passes over the saddle. By holding the shafts steady tugs prevent the vehicle from tipping up or down.

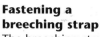

Fastening a breeching strap
The breeching straps pass through metal staples on the shafts, called D rings (or dees), and fasten around the shafts and the traces.

Attaching a trace
The traces are the straps that pull the vehicle. They are attached to the horse's collar at one end and are fastened to hooks at the front of the vehicle on the other end.

Scurry driving

Scurry driving is a type of speed driving competition in which small ponies, such as Shetlands, excel. Contestants are timed as they drive around an obstacle course, often leaning at alarmingly sharp angles as they go around corners.

Holding reins and whip

Your left hand holds both reins, as shown above, with the left rein on the top. Your right hand holds the whip.

Turning

If they hold the reins as shown above (left rein between the thumb and index finger; right rein between the middle and ring fingers), an experienced person can turn a driven horse to the right by turning their left hand so that the palm faces upward. This puts more tension on the right rein and less on the left. In order to turn left, the palm of the hand faces downward, tightening the left rein and releasing the right rein.

Turning left
When you are learning how to drive—or if you just need a stronger aid—your right hand can reinforce the pressure on the left rein, holding it just in front of the left hand.

Using a whip

When driving, your voice and the whip tell the horse to move forward. The whip should just touch it lightly between the collar and the saddle.

Turning right
In order to give a stronger aid for turning right, you use your right hand to put direct pressure on the right rein. Your right hand should not move too far away from your left hand.

Harnesses and vehicles

Harness and vehicles vary according to the purpose for which they are used. A pony pulling a fast, lightweight vehicle, such as a gig, wears a lighter harness than a horse pulling a heavy coach. The harness may use either a neck collar or a breast collar, and it can be decorated with metal fittings. Horses and ponies are usually harnessed singly, in twos (side by side as a pair or one behind the other as a tandem), or in fours.

Browband
This elegant show bridle has a brass-mounted browband.

Rosette
This is a metal button at the end of the browband that occasionally bears the owner's crest or monogram.

Saddle
The padded driving saddle protects the pony's back from the weight of the vehicle that is carried there.

Traces
The traces pull the vehicle.

Hames
Hames are metal arms that fit around the collar. This is where the traces are attached.

Collar
The pony takes the vehicle's weight on its shoulders through the collar.

Girth
The girth holds the saddle firmly in place.

Driving bridle and Liverpool bit

A driving bridle usually has blinkers to prevent the horse from seeing—and being frightened by—the vehicle behind it. The Liverpool bit (left) has three rein positions. The top on the ring is the mildest, and the bottom is the most severe.

Trandem

A team of three horses harnessed beside one another is called a trandem and is rarely seen. The horses shown here are Shires.

Reins
The reins pass through terrets (rings) on the hames and the saddle.

Breeching
The breeching, which is attached to the shafts, allows the pony to stop the vehicle.

Stick-back gig

In the 1800s gigs were a popular form of transportation. Today they are often used by private driving enthusiasts. Lightweight and elegant, they can be pulled by a single pony or a pair.

Royal coach

This splendid ceremonial coach, seen here at the Royal Windsor Horse Show in England, is owned by Queen Elizabeth II. The horses' harnesses and the men's uniforms are elegantly decorated.

Specially trained horses

Police horses—and those used for military ceremonies— go through special training after they have been broken in. Police horses in London, England, start between the ages of five and seven years old. Each horse spends six months "at school," learning not to be afraid of loud noises, waving flags, and unruly crowds. This is followed by six months on patrol with an experienced horse.

Police horses in the U.S.

Controlling crowds in cities is everyday work for police horses all around the world. In many places, including Great Britain, horses doing similar work wear protective guards over their eyes and heads.

Drum horse

Drum horses are always heavy horses because they must carry a rider plus two drums, which weigh almost 60 lbs. (27kg) each. The drummer controls his horse with foot reins.

King's Troop Royal Horse Artillery

The King's Troop Royal Horse Artillery carries out ceremonial duties in Great Britain such as firing royal salutes and providing gun carriages and black horses for state funerals. They are famous for their "Musical Drive"— the climax of which is the amazing "scissor" movement, in which teams of galloping horses pulling gun carriages cross in the middle of the arena with split-second timing.

Parade duty

Part of a London police horse's duties is to escort military bands in ceremonial parades. An untrained horse would be upset by the noise, but a police horse is calm and unruffled.

Ring of fire

Jumping through a flaming hoop is one of the most spectacular parts of a police horse display. The horses are first trained to jump over the box alone, and then they jump over the box through the hoop. Next only part of the hoop is lit. An experienced horse gives a lead.

Glossary

The horse and pony world has a language of its own, and you might not understand all the words you read and hear. This list explains what some of these words mean.

action The way a horse or pony moves.

aids The signals that a rider uses to tell a horse what to do. Natural aids are the rider's legs, **seat**, hands, and voice. Artificial aids include **crops** and spurs.

American barn A stable design used in the U.S. in which a large barn is divided into several **box stalls** on either side of a central aisle.

approach The last few **strides** a horse or a pony takes before a jump.

backing Getting onto a horse for the first time.

balance A horse is balanced when its weight and that of its rider are distributed so that the horse can move easily and efficiently.

bit The part of a bridle that fits in a horse's mouth— usually made out of steel.

blaze A white mark down the front of a horse's face.

boarding barn Keeping a horse or pony on someone else's premises and paying them to look after it for you.

body brush A short-bristled brush used for removing dirt and grease from a horse's or pony's coat.

body protector A stiff vest that helps protect your upper body.

bone The measurement around the **cannon bone**, just below the **knee**. "Plenty of bone" means a high measurement and therefore strong legs.

bounce fence A combination fence with no **stride** between the two elements. A horse lands after one and immediately takes off again for the other.

box stall A stable in which a horse is free to move around.

breastplate A strap that goes around a horse's neck and fastens to the front of the saddle and to the **girth**. It prevents the saddle from slipping backward.

breeching Part of a driving **harness** that helps the horse stop the vehicle it is pulling.

breeching strap a) The strap that attaches the **breeching** to the shafts. b) A strap that is fastened across the back of a trailer to stop a horse from moving backward.

breed association An organization that regulates the breeding of a particular breed of horse or pony.

bridoon A **snaffle bit** used with a **double bridle**.

browband The part of a bridle that fits around a horse's or pony's forehead and stops the **headpiece** from slipping backward.

bucking When a horse kicks out its back legs with its head down or jumps into the air with all four feet off of the ground and its back arched.

cannon bone The bone in the foreleg between the **knee** and the **fetlock**.

cantle The back of a saddle.

cavesson a) A type of **noseband**. b) A halter with swivel rings to which a lunge **rein** is attached.

chaff Chopped hay and straw that is mixed with other feed to stop horses from eating it too quickly.

changing the rein Changing the direction in which you are riding in the **arena** or show ring.

chaps Leather or suede trousers worn over pants to protect the rider's legs.

cheeks a) The flat sides of a horse's face. b) The vertical side parts of a **curb bit**.

cheekpiece The part of a bridle that supports the **bit**.

cinch The **girth** on a western saddle.

clean-legged Legs that carry no **feather**.

clenches The ends of horseshoe nails that are hammered down to hold the shoe in place.

clipping Removing a horse's or pony's winter coat to enable it to work without sweating excessively.

coarse mix A type of prepared **concentrated feed** in which various ingredients are mixed together.

cob A short-legged, small, stocky horse, usually with a **quiet temperament**. The mane is often **roached**.

colic Abdominal pain. Colic can be very serious and needs veterinary attention.

collar Part of a driving **harness** that rests on a horse's shoulders.

collection Moving with shorter, more elevated **strides**, thus shortening the horse's or pony's **outline**.

colt A male horse under the age of four years old.

competition horse A horse that takes part in competitions, usually **eventing**, **dressage**, reining, or **show jumping**.

concentrated feeds Corn, pellets, and **coarse mixes** fed to a horse in small quantities.

concentrates The grains, such as oats and barley, that make up **concentrated feeds**.

conformation The overall shape and proportions of a horse or pony.

contact The link through the **reins** between a horse's mouth and its rider's **hands**.

crest The center of the arch on the **top line** of the neck.

crop A device used to urge on a horse.

cross-country A riding course with jumps that must be completed within a specified time. Cross-country is part of **eventing**.

croup The highest point of the hindquarters.

curb bit A **bit** with **cheeks** and a curb chain that acts on a horse's head and chin as well as his mouth.

curry comb a) A metal comb on a wooden handle

used for cleaning a **body brush**. b) A plastic or rubber version that can be used on a horse or pony to remove mud and loose hairs from its coat.

dandy brush A wooden-backed brush with long, stiff bristles used for removing dried mud and for grooming a pasture-kept pony.

deep litter A system of stable management in which only the droppings are removed in the daily mucking out, and fresh bedding is placed on top of the old.

deep through the girth Deep and broad through the chest and behind the elbows. This gives a lot of space for the heart and lungs.

diagonal a) A pair of a horse's legs diagonally opposite each other (e.g. left fore, right hind). b) A slanting line across an **arena**.

dished face A face that is concave (that curves inward), like the Arabian's.

dishing When a horse moves by throwing its front feet out to the sides instead of going straight; a fault in its action.

disunited Cantering with one leg leading in front and the opposite leg leading behind.

DIY board A way of keeping a horse at a **boarding barn**, where the owner visits every day and does all the work.

dock The area under the top of a horse's tail and the top part of the tail itself.

double bridle A type of bridle with two **bits**.

draft horse A big, heavy horse used for pulling loads or farm implements.

dressage The advanced **schooling** and training of a horse, performed in competitions.

dropped noseband A **noseband** that fastens under the **bit**, preventing a horse from opening its mouth to avoid the action of the bit.

eel stripe A dark stripe along a horse's or pony's back, from its mane to its tail. Seen on Asiatic breeds, as well as Fjord and Highland ponies.

eventing A competition including **dressage**, **cross-country**, and **show jumping**.

extension Moving with longer, lower **strides**, thus lengthening a horse's or pony's **outline**.

feather The long hair that grows on the lower part of the legs of most heavy horses and some ponies.

fender A leather flap that covers the stirrup leather on a western saddle.

fetlock The joint on the lower part of a horse's leg, just above the foot.

filly A female horse under the age of four years old.

flat work schooling training on the ground, not over fences.

flying change Changing the **leading leg** at canter when a horse has all four feet off of the ground.

foal A horse or pony under the age of one year old.

forage Food for a horse or pony, especially grass, hay, and **haylage**.

forehand The head, neck, shoulders, **withers**, and forelegs of a horse or pony.

forelock The part of a horse's or pony's mane that falls over its forehead.

four-beat gait One in which each foot hits the ground separately such as the walk.

frog The V-shaped structure in the sole of a horse's foot.

full board Keeping a horse or pony at a **boarding barn**, where the stable staff carry out all the work involved.

gait The **pace** at which a horse or pony moves. The natural gaits are walk, trot, canter, and gallop.

gaited An American term describing a horse that can perform more gaits than the natural ones. Horses may be three-gaited or five-gaited.

gamgee Raw cotton lined with gauze, used as a padding under leg bandages.

gelding A castrated male horse or pony. He is not able to breed.

gig A lightweight, two-wheeled, horse-drawn vehicle that seats two people.

girth The broad strap that goes around a horse's belly to hold the saddle in place.

going The condition of the ground for riding—wet ground is described as soft or heavy going; dry ground is described as hard going.

grass livery Keeping a horse or pony out in the grass at a **boarding barn**.

grazing rotation Grazing a pasture with cattle and sheep after horses to even out the pasture and prevent the buildup of worm eggs.

gymkhana Mounted games and races usually performed as part of a show.

hack a) To go out for a ride. b) A type of horse suitable for riding.

hackamore A type of bitless bridle.

halfbred A horse or pony with one **Thoroughbred** parent.

half-seat position Leaning forward with the seat off of the saddle and taking the weight on the knees and feet, used when galloping and jumping.

hands a) The units used to measure a horse's height. One hand equals 4 in. (10cm). b) A rider who has light but positive control of the **reins** is said to have good hands.

harness The equipment used on a horse that is being driven. "In harness" means being driven.

haylage Vacuum-packed, partly dried hay. It is dust free and fed to horses with breathing problems.

headpiece The part of a bridle or halter that goes over the horse's head.

hh Stands for "hands high."

horse An equine animal that stands 14.3 **hands** (59 in. or 150cm) high or taller.

hunter A horse used for hunting. It must be able to gallop and jump well.

hunting cap A velvet-covered hard riding hat with a brim.

impulsion The energy a rider creates in a horse by the use of the legs and **seat**.

in hand Leading a horse or pony while on foot.

inbred Bred from animals that are closely related to each other.

jog a) A slow trot. b) A **gait** in western riding.

jump off An extra round or rounds used to decide the winner in **show jumping** when two or more competitors have the same score.

keeper A small loop on a strap through which the end

is put to keep it flat and neat.

knee The joint halfway down the foreleg.

laminitis A painful inflammation of the inside of a horse's hooves, usually caused by overfeeding.

landing The stage of a jump when the horse's feet touch the ground again.

lateral At the side. A lateral **gait** is when both legs on the same side move together.

leading file The horse and rider at the front of a group.

leading leg The leg that is in front of the others when a horse is cantering.

leg into hand A riding term meaning that you can create energy in a horse or pony by using your legs and can control it using your **hands**.

leg up An easy way of mounting a horse in which a helper holds the rider's left leg and helps him or her jump up onto the saddle.

Liverpool bit A driving **bit** with three different rein positions.

loading Putting a horse into a trailer.

long-reining Driving a horse while on foot.

lungeing Exercising a horse on a long rein that is attached to a special halter. The horse is asked to walk, trot, and canter in circles.

manège An enclosed arena used for riding and **schooling**.

mare A female horse or pony aged four years old or more.

markings, record of A horse's or pony's markings are recorded on vaccination certificates and passports.

martingale A piece of **tack** designed to stop a horse from throwing its head up too high. A standing martingale runs from the **noseband** to the **girth**; a running martingale from the **reins** to the girth.

mealy Light colored, the color of oatmeal.

mowing a pasture Cutting down weeds and long, coarse grasses to improve grazing.

muzzle The area around a horse's mouth.

native pony A pony breed, such as Exmoor, Welsh, or Highland, that was bred on the moors and mountains of Great Britain.

near side The left side of a horse or pony.

neck strap A strap that passes around a horse's neck either a) for a rider to hold onto or b) as part of a **martingale** or **breastplate**.

neck-reining A way of turning used in western riding in which both **reins** are held in one hand.

Norfolk Trotter A fast-trotting harness horse that existed between the 1400s and mid-1900s; ancestor of the Hackney Horse and others.

noseband The part of a bridle that goes around a horse's or pony's nose.

novice An inexperienced rider or horse.

off side The right side of a horse or pony.

on the bit A horse's head held in a position in which the rider has the maximum control of it.

outline The shape a horse's or pony's body makes when it is being ridden.

overface To ask a horse to do work, such as jumping, which is beyond its current stage of training.

pace a) Another word for **gait**. b) A specific gait in which a horse moves both legs on one side together.

pack pony A pony that carries heavy loads in packs that are strapped to its back.

partbred A horse or pony that has one **purebred** parent or two purebred parents of different breeds.

part-colored When a horse is more than one color such as skewbald.

pastern The part of a horse's leg between the foot and the **fetlock** joint.

pasture shelter A shed with an open front in a pasture that provides horses and ponies with some protection from the weather.

pedigree A table that lists an animal's parents, grandparents, great-grandparents, etc.

pelham A type of **bit** with two **reins** and a curb chain.

plain head An unattractive or ugly head.

point of the shoulder The front of the shoulder joint where the shoulder blade joins the first bone of the animal's foreleg.

points a) The physical features of a horse. b) Areas on a horse that are described as part of its color. A horse with "black points" (usually a bay or a dun) has a black mane, tail, and lower legs.

pommel The front part of a saddle.

pony An equine animal that stands up to 14.2 **hands** (57 in. or 147cm) high.

ponylike head A small, neat head with small ears and large eyes.

port A raised, half-moon shape in the mouthpiece of a **curb bit** that allows room for a horse's tongue.

presence The way that a horse or pony carries itself.

primitive When it is used to describe a breed, "primitive" means at an early stage of evolution.

pulling a mane and tail Pulling out a few long hairs to neaten the appearance of a mane and tail.

purebred A horse or pony that has two parents of the same breed **registered** in the breed's **stud book**.

putting to Harnessing a horse to a vehicle.

quarter marks Decorative patterns made on the **quarters** by brushing against the lie of the coat with a damp brush.

quartering A quick brushing done before exercising a horse or pony.

quarters The area of a horse behind the saddle—its hindquarters and hindlegs.

quick-release knot A knot that can be undone quickly by pulling one end of the rope. Used to tie up horses and haynets.

quiet Describes a calm horse that is not easily upset.

rack A fast **gait** in which each foot hits the ground separately.

ragwort A yellow-flowered plant that is highly poisonous to horses and other animals.

registered Listed in the **stud book** of the breed to which the horse or pony belongs. A registered horse has a **pedigree**.

rein back Stepping

backward. The horse's legs move in **diagonal** pairs.

reins The parts of a bridle that run from the **bit** to the rider's hands.

rhythm The evenness and regularity of a horse's or pony's hoof beats.

roaching Cutting off a horse's or pony's mane.

roller A broad band that fastens around a horse's belly to hold a blanket in place.

Roman nose A nose that, seen in profile, is convex, or curves outward.

running out When a horse or pony refuses to jump over a fence by going around the side of it.

saddle pad A saddle-shaped pad used under a saddle to prevent it from rubbing and to absorb a horse's sweat.

safety harness The adjustable straps that hold a helmet in position.

safety vest A vest worn over riding clothes to warn motorists of a rider's presence or that the horse is nervous or inexperienced.

schooling Training a horse.

schooling helmet A hard, brimless hat used for riding.

seat a) A rider's position in the saddle. b) The part of the saddle on which a rider sits.

showing Exhibiting a horse or pony at a horse show, where it is judged on its **conformation** and **gait**.

show jumping A jumping competition at a horse show.

shying Jumping sideways when startled.

side reins **Reins** that run from the **bit** to a **surcingle**.

skipping out Collecting droppings from a stable in a bucket.

sloping shoulders Shoulders that slope from the **withers** to the **point of the shoulder**. They give smooth, comfortable **gaits** in a riding horse.

sluggish Describes a lazy pony that is reluctant to work.

snaffle bit A **bit** that is usually jointed in the center and has two rings.

solid color The same color all over, with markings only on the legs and face.

sound A "sound" horse is a healthy one, with no lameness or breathing problems.

Spanish Horse The most important European breed of horse for centuries, which had a huge impact on horse breeding throughout the world. Most American breeds are descended from the Spanish Horse.

spread fence A wide fence where the back part is higher than the front part.

stable stains Marks on a stabled horse caused by lying in dirty bedding.

stallion A male horse or pony, aged four years old or more, used for breeding.

stamina The ability to keep going even when very tired.

standards The sides of a jump.

straight action Moving the legs straight forward and backward without any sideways movement.

strapping Thorough grooming of a stabled horse done after exercise.

stride The distance traveled by a horse's foot between two successive impacts with the ground.

stud book A book in which the name, date of birth, and **pedigree** of a **purebred** horse or pony is **registered**, or listed. Every horse and pony breed has a stud book.

studs Metal pieces screwed into the heels of a horse's shoes to prevent it from slipping.

surcingle A band with rings used to attach side reins.

suspension The moment that all of a horse's feet are off of the ground at the same time when cantering.

sweat scraper Used for removing water from a horse's coat when washing it or sponging it down.

tack All the pieces of saddlery used on a riding horse or pony.

takeoff The stage of a jump when a horse launches itself into the air.

temperament A horse's or pony's nature for example, calm, gentle, or excitable.

thatching Putting straw under a wet horse's blanket to help it dry without getting the blanket wet.

Thoroughbred A breed of horse **registered** in the General **Stud Book**. All racehorses are registered Thoroughbreds.

throatlatch The part of a bridle that goes under the horse's throat and stops the bridle from slipping forward.

top line The upper part of a horse's back, from the **withers** to the hindquarters.

trace Part of a driving **harness**; a strap that pulls the vehicle. It runs from the **collar** hames (metal arms) to the vehicle.

transition The change from one **gait** to another.

An upward transition is from a slower to a faster gait; a downward transition is from a faster to a slower gait.

tree The framework on which a saddle is built.

trotting poles Poles set on the ground for training a horse or rider to jump.

tug A leather loop through which the shaft of a vehicle passes. Tugs prevent it from tipping up or down.

turn out To let a horse loose in a pasture.

under saddle When a horse or pony is ridden.

uneven ground Ground that is cut up and muddy.

up to weight Capable of carrying a heavy rider.

upright shoulders Shoulders that do not slope very much from the **withers** to the **point of the shoulder**. They are better for carrying a **harness** collar.

vaulting a) Jumping up onto a horse without using the stirrups. b) Gymnastics on horseback.

waist The narrowest part of a saddle's **seat**.

water brush A short-bristled brush used when damp to lay the mane and tail in place when grooming.

weigh tape A tape wrapped around a horse's **girth** from which you can read its weight.

wind A horse's breathing.

withers The bony ridge at the base of a horse's neck.

worming Giving medicine to kill parasitic worms inside a horse's intestines.

zebra marks Horizontal dark stripes on the legs of **primitive** breeds of ponies.

Index

HORSE AND PONY WEB SITES

www.aqha.com
American Quarter Horse Association

www.equestrian.org
National Equestrian Federation
of the U.S.

www.equiworld.net
International horse and pony
information

www.haynet.net
The Horse Source—directory
of horse-related web sites

www.horsesport.org
Fédération Equestre Internationale—
International Federation of
Equestrian Sport

www.horseworlddata.com
General horse and pony information
for enthusiasts

www.ilph.org
International League for the
Protection of Horses

www.imh.org
International Museum of the
Horse and Kentucky Horse Park
in Lexington, KY

www.nhjc.org
National Hunter and Jumper
Committees of the U.S.

www.ponyclub.org
The official U.S. Pony Club site

www.newrider.com
Advice and information
for new riders

www.youngrider.com
Young Rider magazine

NOTE TO READERS

The web site addresses listed in
this book are correct at the time
of going to print. However, due
to the ever-changing nature of
the Internet, web site addresses
and content can change. Web sites
can contain links that are unsuitable
for children. The publisher cannot
be held responsible for changes in
web site addresses or content or
for information obtained through
third-party web sites. We strongly
advise that Internet searches are
supervised by an adult.

ACKNOWLEDGMENTS

Kingfisher would like to thank:
Inspector Alan Hiscox of the
Metropolitan Police in England;
Dickie Waygood, Riding Master of
the Household Cavalry in England;
Captain Mark Dollar of the
Household Cavalry in England.

Everybody at **The Talland School
of Equitation**, especially the Hutton
family and Patricia Curtis.

Everybody at **Hartpury College
Equestrian Centre**, especially
Margaret Linington-Payne.

Lesley Ward, the founder and
editor of *Young Rider* magazine, for
her invaluable assistance with the
American edition of this book.

Models:
Tom Alexander
Alison Jane Berman
Anna Bird
Emily Brady
Blake Christian
James Cole
Emily Coles
Patricia Curtis
Wesley Davis
Sam Drinkwater
Parker Dunn
Amelia Ebanks
Naomi Ebanks
Theo Freyne
Helen Grundy
Sarah Grundy
Simon Grundy
Emma Harford
Brian Hutton
Charlie Hutton
Pippa Hutton
Hannah James
Pete Jenkins (equine dentist)
Olivia Kuropatwa
Sophie Kuropatwa
Eric Lin
Margaret Linington-Payne
Rhiannon Linington-Payne
Ella McEwan
Thomas McEwen
Lucy Miller (advanced riding)
Charlotte Nagle
Alasdair Nicol
Gemma Oakley
Andrew Poynton (farrier)
Jay Rathore
Nicola Ridley
Ignacio Romero Torres
Ros Sheppard (western riding
    consultant)
Victoria Taylor
Max Thomas (farrier)
Sophie Thomas
Camilla Tracey
Ayako Watanabe
Laura Wilks
Sawako Yoshii

Additional photography by:
Art Archive p10bl, p10c, p10/11t,
p10/11b, p11tr; Houghtons Horses
p31br, p32b, p37tl, p46bl, p50br,
p54bl, p56br, p56bl, p61c, p69tr;
Only Horses Picture Library p36bl,
p43b, p45bl, p65b; Sandy
Felsenthal/CORBIS p214/215b